raising a
christian daughter
in an
mtv
world

raising a christian daughter

in an
mtv
world

Mary Ruth Murdoch

P&R
PUBLISHING
P.O.BOX 817 • PHILLIPSBURG • NEW JERSEY 08865-0817

Page design by Tobias Design
Typesetting by Michelle Feaster

Printed in the United States of America

Library of Congress Cataloging-in-Publication Data

Murdoch, Mary Ruth, 1954-
    Raising a Christian daughter in an MTV world
        p.   cm.
    Includes bibliographical references.
    ISBN 0-87552-373-0 (paperback)
    1. Parenting—Religious aspects—Christianity. 2. Daughters—Religious life. I. Title.
    BV4529.M87 2000
    248.8'45—dc21

                                   00-027433

To Ellie, Sarah, and Annie:

May you grow in wisdom,
knowing what God wants you to know
and doing what God wants you to do.

Contents

Acknowledgments

It was one thing to offer opinions and advice over a cup of tea; it was another to write them down and deliver them to a publisher. That took the insightful advice and persistent nagging of many friends. Thanks go especially to Nancy Strong, Janice Kinneer, Rev. Jack Kinneer, Rev. Erick Allen, and Melissa Craig.

Thanks to Thom Notaro for recognizing the diamond in the rough manuscript and offering many excellent suggestions, and to Barbara Lerch.

Thanks to my parents for your wisdom and good example. Ellie, Sarah, and Annie are your crown, and I am proud to be your daughter (Proverbs 17:6).

Thanks to my husband, John. You are my best friend, a true partner, and a wonderful father of our daughters.

PART 1

The Challenge

Points for Prayer

❦ Thank God for your daughter and the opportunity he has given you to teach her God's ways.

❦ Pray that God would work in your heart and in your daughter's heart.

"Get wisdom, discipline and understanding." —Proverbs 23:23b

CHAPTER 1

What Your Daughter Needs

It's a great time to have a daughter. Her future is full of opportunity. Microwave ovens, vacuum cleaners, automatic washers, dryers, and dishwashers have promised her greater freedom from household chores, and companies continue to develop better and better gadgets. She has more opportunities for education and more options for work. Women make up nearly half the American work force. They own businesses and head Fortune 500 companies. They sit on the Supreme Court and serve on presidential cabinets. Even the workplace has changed. With computers and modems a woman can "e-mail over oatmeal." She can conduct teleconferences from the kitchen table. She can use her talents in more ways than ever before.

Yet, it is a terrifying time to have a daughter. Her world is a more dangerous place than we grew up in. Women are more likely to be single mothers and to live with their children in poverty. They fear rape and domestic violence. They are overworked, stressed, and depressed. They are more preoccupied with physical appearance and more likely to develop eating disorders.

It's a particularly bad time to have a *teenage* daughter. "Adolescence is not an age; it's a disease," my mother-in-law says;

"but fortunately they outgrow it." Only now, many teenage girls are not coming out of it whole.

- About half of girls have had sexual intercourse by age eighteen.[1]
- The average American teen will be sexually active for about eight years before marriage.[2]
- More than half of teenage girls say they would consider having a child out of wedlock.[3]
- One third of illegitimate births are to teenage mothers.[4]
- On average, girls who smoke start at age thirteen, who drink at age fifteen, and who use marijuana at age thirteen.[5]
- Girls between eleven and fifteen are the one group experiencing an increase in eating disorders.[6]
- The psychological problems of adolescents have become more intense and more require medication.[7]
- Forty percent of girls in one midwestern city have considered suicide.[8]

Between childhood and adulthood, girls go through many changes—physically, intellectually, emotionally, and socially. Between elementary school and high school, girls' bodies mature, their emotions fluctuate, their relationships change, their interests ebb and flow. They wonder, *Who am I? What should I do? Where do I fit in?* At the same time, girls face decisions we never had to make at their age. Drugs are readily available, and sex is everywhere: in movies, top 40 songs, their sex education classes, and perhaps even the hallways of their schools.

The junior high school years have become particularly critical for girls, the age at which many "risk behaviors" begin. "Tweens," children ages eight to twelve, are also beginning to show signs of being at risk.

Changing from little girls to teenagers to adults can be rough and stormy. Like sailors rounding the Cape of Good

Hope and caught in the churning waters between the Atlantic Ocean and the Pacific, it can seem they'll never make it to calmer seas. This book is meant to help you and your daughter not only avoid shipwreck but enjoy her journey to becoming a young woman of good character (Prov. 23:15–16, 24–25).

What Your Daughter Needs

Psychologists say that girls need better self-esteem. The Scriptures say that they need training in wisdom, that is, in knowing what God wants them to know and doing what God wants them to do. They need the wisdom that comes only through a personal and saving relationship with Jesus Christ (see Prov. 9:10; 1 Cor. 1:18–2:16).

You, as a Christian parent, are to bring your daughter up in "the training and instruction of the Lord" (Eph. 6:4). "Folly is bound up in the heart of a child"; your job is to drive it far from her, to train her in the way she should go (Prov. 22:6, 15), and to admonish and teach her so that you may present her mature and complete in Christ (Eph. 4:13–15; Col. 1:28; James 1:4–5). This will not happen overnight.

Raising a happy teenage daughter begins the day you bring your baby girl home from the hospital or the adoption agency. The relationship and influence you have with her when she is thirteen depends on how you teach her when she is two, and six, and ten. You don't have to dread your daughter's teen years, but you do have to prepare for them, and the earlier you start, the better. This doesn't mean that if your daughter is already fifteen, it is automatically too late. In discipline, "there is hope" (Prov. 19:18).

A happy daughter requires two ingredients: parents who have trained her in wisdom and a daughter who has learned to practice wisdom. Many teenage girls are in big trouble because parents have let them make their own decisions without preparing them to make good decisions. They have left them with hearts untrained in God's ways.

Where Have All the Parents Gone?

The after-school hours have become the unsupervised hours. More teenage girls are getting pregnant at three in the afternoon in their own homes than at ten at night in the back seat of the Chevy. More teenage crime is being committed after school than after midnight. In more families, both parents work outside the home, and more children than ever are on their own after school—and they are not using the time wisely.

Where are the parents? This is a larger question than whether both parents work or how many adults it takes to supervise teen parties. The real question is what role parents should play in their children's lives.

Child psychologists have focused on how to make children feel good about themselves. How can a daughter become an interesting and unique adult if she is always being told no? Rules stifle creativity. She should make her own choices and learn from her own mistakes.

So we're told. No wonder parents feel they have lost control of their children. They don't like what their children are doing, but they dare not say no. They worry, *How will she react? What will it do to her self-esteem? Will we dampen her spirit?*

Christian parents have a blueprint for developing their daughter's good character. The Bible tells parents what behavior to encourage and discourage. It tells your daughter who she is and what she should do. It says that true freedom and fulfillment come from Jesus Christ (John 8:31–36; 10:10b), that our biggest fear should be of the One who can destroy body and soul in hell (Matt. 10:28), and that a parent who doesn't discipline a child is a willing partner to her death (Prov. 19:18), but discipline saves her soul (23:13–14). Your most important parental responsibility is caring for your daughter's soul by helping her know what Jesus wants her to know, and do what Jesus wants her to do.

"I Mighta Been Somebody . . ."

Marlon Brando's character looks back with regret on wasted opportunities: "I coulda been a contenduh." But wasted opportunities don't happen just in movies.

Angela studied hard in high school and planned to go to college in the fall, but over the summer she moved in with her boyfriend. Before long, she was pregnant. She never went to college.

Fifteen-year-old Mary was worried about her friend, who owed a drug dealer $300. He was threatening to kill her if she didn't pay up. Mary didn't want her friend to meet the drug dealer alone, and so she went along. The drug dealer shot them both and left them to bleed to death by the side of the road.

Though one bad decision changed each of these lives, their stories really began years earlier. Often parents don't pay attention to the small choices their daughters make, but those decisions set them on a course toward wisdom or foolishness, toward obedience or disobedience to God, toward reliance on Jesus or rejection of him. "Way leads on to way."[9]

"I guess you just get into the wrong crowd. You go in with your eyes closed. You think it's fun at first; then it becomes a way of life," Kim said at her cousin's funeral. Carol had been a promising student and musician, but then she began using drugs. When she was a teenager, she took up prostitution to pay for her habit. "She was on a path of self-destruction and I knew it was going to end soon," said her lawyer. At twenty-nine, she was found beaten and strangled beside the road.[10]

On the other hand, Sunni grew up in a Christian home and learned to serve God early in life. When she was a teenager, she started playing the piano for our church. She graduated from a Christian college and went to work as a hospital dietitian. At twenty-nine, she married a young man who wants to be a pastor.

How your daughter's life turns out will be the result of the decisions she makes—large and small—decisions that grow out of her relationship with God. If she has learned to love and obey God, she will make wise choices. If she has not, she will make foolish ones. Foolish choices result in wasted lives and regrets (Prov. 5:11–14).

It can be terrifying that part of your daughter's growing up is her becoming a separate person from you. You can't make her have faith in God or compel her every decision. Some of the decisions she makes you will never even know about. Did you tell your parents everything you did? Neither will your daughter. Sooner or later, your daughter must take responsibility for her own direction in life and make her own choices. She must decide whether she will love God and keep his commands.

She will love him and keep his commands if he has changed her heart. This inner work is God's (2 Thess. 2:13–14; 1 Peter 1:1–2), and yet, in a way we can't fully understand, you become part of that work (Col. 1:28–29). God uses you to help form your daughter's good character through your teaching, discipline, example, and prayers.

A daughter of noble character is worth far more than rubies (Prov. 31:10). To help form your daughter's good character, you need to know what you're up against, including what she is hearing about herself, about sex and marriage, about right and wrong. You need a plan to train her in righteousness and wisdom. She needs to learn what God's Word says about her, her character, and her relationships to others. You need to show her Jesus by the way you live, how you treat her, and what you teach her. Above all, you need to pray that God would change her from within.

My Three Girls

Our eldest daughter, Ellie, reached the teenage milestone a few years ago. The road hasn't been without bumps. We have had many emotional late-night talks in her bedroom and serious conversations in the car. Sometimes she displays the foolishness of the young. Yet, Ellie is a joy to her parents as she develops into a responsible young woman, showing the fruits of good character and growing in love for and obedience to Jesus.

Our second daughter, Sarah, is leaving that in-between stage, when life is peaceful and parents can be lulled into thinking, *Our daughter is civilized.* Not yet! Sarah's faith in Jesus has yet to be challenged by serious peer pressure, but she is showing signs of "middle school syndrome"—the delightful and sometimes scary *changes* girls undergo at that age.

Our youngest daughter, Annie, has Down syndrome, and she needs a lot of what her preschool teacher called "behavior management." What worked with her sisters often doesn't work with her, but her faith in Jesus is developing with her mental abilities.

You will find in this book what we have been teaching our three daughters—around the dinner table, during trips in the car, while staying up late to talk over their problems and daydreams, by the example we set for them, and in the way we treat them.

Each chapter begins with points for prayer. Throughout this book, you will find applications suggesting topics for family devotions, discussions to have with your daughter, or Scripture verses for her to memorize. Some of the questions for further thought and discussion also would be appropriate in family devotions or could be adapted as individual Bible studies for your daughter.

Your daughter need not become another statistic like the ones on page 4. Even if she does fall into the sins described there, that need not be the end of the story. God's promises give us hope: "Train a child in the way she should go and when she is old, she will not turn from it" (Prov. 22:6 paraphrased). "The promise of God is for you and your children and for all who are far off—for all whom the Lord our God will call" (Acts 2:39). "He tends his flock like a shepherd: He gathers the lambs in his arms and carries them close to his heart; he gently leads those that have young" (Isa. 40:11).

God offers himself to you and to your daughter. By his grace, you can be a faithful parent, and because of his grace, you can have hope that your daughter will learn to love God and live for him.

For Further Thought and Discussion

1. Read Proverbs 9:10 and 1 Corinthians 1:18–2:16. Why does true wisdom come only to those who have a personal and saving relationship with Jesus Christ? How will this wisdom affect the decisions we make? Why does your daughter need this kind of wisdom?
2. Read Proverbs 19:18; 23:13–14; and Matthew 10:28. What should be our greatest fear? What is your greatest responsibility in raising your daughter? Why?
3. Read Galatians 5:22–23; Ephesians 2:10; Philippians 2:12–13; Colossians 1:28–29; 2 Thessalonians 2:13–14; and 1 Peter 1:2. Who produces the fruit of good character? How do parents become part of this work? How does your daughter? How, then, should you pray?

Points for Prayer

🎕 Pray that God would keep your daughter safe from temptation.

🎕 Pray that God would renew your daughter with the mind of Christ.

*"Do not conform any longer to the pattern of this world,
but be transformed by the renewing of your mind." —Romans 12:2*

CHAPTER 2

Your Daughter and the World

My husband is a founding member of the Secret Council of Fathers of Daughters.

Not long after our first daughter was born, our friends adopted a daughter. Over dinner one night, we talked about how life had changed since we had become parents. Having been teenage boys, my husband, John, and our friend Jack worried about the day when their precious daughters would begin to date *boys*. They wanted a defense against that dreaded day. Their first idea was that, of course, there would be no trouble—they would simply go along, in the back seat. Soon, however, they devised another plan, and thus began the Secret Council of Fathers of Daughters.

What does the Secret Council of Fathers of Daughters do? Each member periodically threatens single, unattached males. It doesn't matter whether they are actual or even potential boyfriends. On general principle, single, unattached males are the enemies of fathers of daughters. In the event a daughter ever does go out on a date, the father should so scare the boy that there will be absolutely no reason to worry about what goes on during the date. Jack's scenario for Aileen's first date went something like this:

JACK (*cleaning his collection of firearms*): Good evening, son. Come in. Sit down.

(*Boy sits down across from Jack.*)

JACK: Son, I love my daughter. [*Pause.*] I would die for my daughter. [*Pause. Looks up at boy.*] And I would kill for my daughter. [*Smiles.*] Have a good time!

Jack figured the boy would get the idea.

Actually, the Secret Council of Fathers of Daughters is mostly tongue-in-cheek. Our daughters' best protection from sexual sin, drugs, alcohol, fast cars, and fast boys is knowing what God wants them to know and doing what God wants them to do. "How can a young woman keep her way pure? By living according to your word. If she seeks you with all her heart, you will not let her stray from your commands. She will hide your word in her heart that she might not sin against you" (Ps. 119:9–11 paraphrased). Regardless of how well we try to protect them, our daughters will

- hear language we don't use,
- learn ideas we don't teach,
- see movies at someone else's house,
- hear music with raunchy lyrics,
- know who sells drugs,
- feel pressured to engage in sexual activity,
- see the way others live,
- be in situations we can't control,
- make decisions without consulting us.

We can't be with our daughters all the time. Of course, we could just lock them up and stand guard. At times I have felt this would be a really good idea, but it is not very practical. Someone still has to go to the grocery store, buy clothes, fill the car with gasoline, pay the mortgage. Even if we could keep them away from the bad influences of the world outside, they would still find sin in their own homes, because we are all sinners. There is nowhere to hide. We and our daughters can't retreat; we must train them in wisdom. We want our children to grow up physically, mentally, spiritually, and socially, as Jesus did (Luke 2:52). We want them to become wise adults.

So then, we are in the world—and so are our daughters. God leaves us here to be witnesses to our neighbors (Matt. 28:18–20; John 17:21), the salt of the earth, the light of the world, a city on a hill (Matt. 5:13–16). But at least one survey showed virtually no difference between young people in evangelical churches and the general population: they engage in sexual behaviors, use violence, and lie just about as often as their peers.[1] Instead of influencing the world, they have absorbed the world's ways, attitudes, and values.

When the World Talks . . .

The world delivers temptations as irresistible as a slow pitch in the middle of the strike zone. We want to follow the world's ways just as we want to swing at that pitch. Our own sinful desires predispose us to like the world's ways better than God's. The theme of the world is "Do what you want to do," and it has been since the Garden of Eden.

In the Garden, the Serpent tempted Eve to do what she wanted rather than what God commanded. He persuaded her to forget about the consequences and make her own choice. He convinced her that God was not good and wise but was depriving her of something she really should have (Gen. 3:1–5). Our daughters hear the same from their peers, from movies, from pop songs. They read it in books and magazines and off billboards: "God doesn't really mean you shouldn't do *that.*" "Think of all you're missing out on." "You have the right to do what you decide." "Who's to say what's right or wrong?" "If it feels good, just do it." "Indulge yourself." "Nothing bad will happen."

Satan makes sin seem attractive by distorting and misusing the truth (see Luke 4:1–13), and there is often distorted truth in what our daughters hear: "Sex is fun." "Women are just like men." "You should be attractive." Messages like these are dangerous precisely because we can find them true, in a certain sense. We need to ask, "Fun when and at what cost?" "Equal how?" "Attractive in what way?"

You can help your daughter resist the world by teaching her to evaluate everything she reads and hears by what the Bible says about it. When is sex fun as God intended it to be? Show her Proverbs 5. When is sex foolish and harmful? Show her Proverbs 6 and 7. Have her memorize Proverbs 9:17–18: " 'Stolen water is sweet; food eaten in secret is delicious!' But little do they know that the dead are there, that her guests are in the depths of the grave."

When the world talks, we don't just listen; we interact. If we're not careful, we begin to think as the world does. The more we think as the world does, the more bad choices we make (see Rom. 1:18–32). But the more we are "transformed by the renewing of" our minds, the less we are conformed to the world, and the more we know and do God's will (Rom. 12:2).

Teenage girls are in trouble today because they are thinking as the world thinks about themselves and about what they should do. They are making bad choices because they have gone along with the world's ideas.

Application *In family devotions, read Genesis 3. Ask, How did Satan deceive Eve? What happened because Adam and Eve sinned? Do we hear the same messages today? How can we resist them? Teach your daughter always to ask, What does the Bible say about it?*

You Are What You Hear?

"You'll never make more than minimum wage, and you should be glad to get that because you're stupid. You can't make it without me," Jamey's husband told her time after time. And she believed it. When she first came to our church, she was like a scared little rabbit: she was out the door before anyone could even say hello. But she needed help. Before long, her husband left her and their three children. She needed a new apartment and a better-paying job.

One of the deacons found a job for her and gave her rides to work. Every day, back and forth, he gave her the Jesse Jackson speech: "I am somebody. Repeat after me . . . I am . . . somebody." Along with actually having her say those words, he talked to her about what the Bible says she should do. Gradually, she realized, "Hey, I'm *not* worthless in *God's* sight. I'm his child in Christ. I can do all things through him!" Now, she coordinates the women's ministry, oversees the church nursery, and organizes all the church dinners. I don't know what our church would do without her.

Jamey was transformed into a woman who serves God and his people. You want your daughter to grow into a woman who serves God and his people, too. The real tragedy of our culture is not that girls don't feel good about themselves, but that too many girls do not know themselves in relation to a holy and gracious God and therefore are not glorifying and enjoying him.[2] They are not living in such a way that those around them can see what God is like. They are not content with the way God created them or the circumstances in which he has placed them. And they are not doing the work God gave them to do because they think as the world does.

What we hear and read and see has power to influence us. Girls in our culture hear, read, and see "You're a bubblehead," "You're a sex object," "You don't need marriage." And too many of them believe it. They absorb the world's attitudes and values as "must's," "ought's," "should's," and "gotta's": "I must be thin to be attractive." "I ought to have sex like everyone else." "I should be popular." "I gotta be cool." They become what they hear.

Let's take a closer look at what they hear from our culture and how they respond.

Culture: "You're a Bubblehead"

The core of the bubblehead message is that women aren't as smart as men, that women are not really competent to deal with life's demands, that women are not strong enough—physically, mentally, or emotionally. This is why a woman needs a man.

The other side of the message is that men want bubblehead women. So then, if a woman is actually talented, intelligent, and competent, around men she should pretend that she is not.

Girl: "I Can't Compete with Boys." Before junior high, girls see themselves as equal to boys. They compete with boys in sports and expect to win. They don't worry that earning better grades than boys will make them unpopular. They delight in anything that pits the boys against the girls, whether soccer or spelling.

Junior high brings more than a change in school buildings. Girls become acutely aware of the differences between boys and girls. It is during adolescence that girls are especially vulnerable to the bubblehead message. They feel uncomfortable with their developing bodies, insecure about their changing relationships with boys, and unsure about their own abilities. They are young enough and foolish enough (see Prov. 22:15) to "reason emotionally": if they *feel* something is true, it must be true. Their emotions are erratic and intense, and their thinking is immature. One minute they think they can take on the world, and the next minute, they are in despair. While they are learning to reason abstractly, they still see things in black and white. They have trouble putting things in perspective.

Teenage girls have more than just a logical-emotional problem, however. In junior high, boys actually do become stronger than girls. In seventh grade Ellie could beat the strongest boy in her class in arm wrestling; by the beginning of eighth grade he beat her, and by the end of eighth grade, she lost to all the boys. There is a reason boys and girls don't play on the same teams in junior high. This weakness compared to boys is another reason girls think they have less ability.

When girls adopt the bubblehead message, they stop trying

to be the best they can be. Some of them really believe they have less ability than boys; others figure that they will be more popular if they *act* as if they have less ability. Girls who don't use their abilities are not just shortchanging themselves or society. They are shortchanging the God who made them and to whom they owe good and faithful service (see Matt. 25:14–30).

Girl: "I Need a Boyfriend." "I don't feel good about myself unless a guy likes me," said a fourteen-year-old girl. One Saturday, she told her parents she was at a sleep-over with girl friends but spent the night at a hotel with a boy.[3]

Even in elementary school, Marie rarely talked about anything but boys. When one relationship broke up, it was never long before she had another boyfriend, and her choices seemed to go from bad to worse. Before she turned sixteen, she was pregnant.

Pam was intelligent, attractive, and outgoing. But she had a boyfriend who regularly beat her up. Even though Pam appeared confident, she was insecure without a boyfriend.

Each of these girls made bad decisions because each thought, *I need a boyfriend to be somebody.* They searched for acceptance in the wrong places and from the wrong people. When girls look for acceptance in the wrong places, they break the first commandment to worship and serve God alone. They want to please others more than to please God. They commit sexual sin to keep a boyfriend, smoke or take drugs to fit in with the crowd, dress provocatively, cut school, disobey parents. They do not stand up to their peers and do what is right.

Application *Teach your daughter the first commandment and that it means knowing and serving God as the only true God and not putting anyone or anything else before him. Have her memorize the answers to questions 45–48 of the Westminster Shorter Catechism.[4] Teach her that putting God first means pleasing God instead of people. Have her memorize Acts 5:29: "We must obey God rather than men!"*

Culture: "You're a Sex Object"

What is the chief end of woman? For a large part of our culture, the chief end of woman is to attract a man and hold onto him forever. So she wears short skirts and tight blouses. She spends hours on her face and hair. She wears high heels because they make her legs appear longer and more shapely—and visits her podiatrist regularly. She has liposuction, breast implants, a nose job, or a face lift to look younger and more attractive. She will do anything to stay thin. She colors her gray hair. Age is her enemy, because she must hold her man through sheer physical attraction.

Girl: "I Must Look Like a Model." "In all the years I've been a therapist, I've yet to meet one girl who likes her body. . . . When I speak to classes, I ask any woman in the audience who feels good about her body to come up afterward. . . . I have yet to have a woman come up."[5] Girls think that the most important thing about them is their physical appearance. But not even the Playmate of the Month looks like her own picture in real life without the make-up, lighting, and, these days, computer enhancing. No wonder so many teenagers dislike their bodies.

The typical model is both taller and thinner than the average woman. The average woman looks at herself in the mirror—and starts another diet. Glenn Frey sings,

> It's the same sad story all over the world;
> Every man is looking for the perfect girl.
> He sees her every day in a magazine;
> Sees her every night on the TV screen.
> Something is wrong with this picture.[6]

Something *is* wrong with this picture when girls as young as nine diet, and millions of women in America have eating disorders.

When girls focus on outward appearance, they usually neglect inner character. They are less likely to serve God and more likely to be self-absorbed.

Girl: "Just Say Yes." Joanna came home from school one day and showed her mother a piece of paper she had gotten in her sex education class. It showed a diving board and the slogan "Having sex is like going off a diving board." The rest of the sheet explained how, just like the first time you go off a diving board, you might not like sex the first time. Of course, the point of this handout was to convince teenage girls to have sex, regardless of their fears or discomfort. Instead of helping girls to say no, this teacher was pushing them to say yes.

"Your hormones are raging." "Sex is a need, just like food and water." "You don't need to wait for marriage." "We know you'll have sex anyway; just be sure and use birth control." What do girls hear? "We expect you to have sex before marriage."

About half of teenage girls *are* having sex before marriage. And one result of just saying yes is the astounding numbers of illegitimate children.

Culture: "We Don't Need Marriage"

The "sexual revolution" could never have succeeded without birth control pills. For the first time, women had access to a birth control method that was so highly effective, they had virtually no fear of pregnancy from sexual activity. It was "no-fault sex."

At the same time, young people were rejecting traditions and parental values. Feminists were telling women that marriage was repressive and unnecessary and that society was sexist because it held to a double standard. Feminists said, "If men can do it, so can women."

When feminists said, "Women are exploited by marriage," "All the differences between men and women are cultural, so women should act just like men," and "Don't ever really trust a man," they hastened along today's family disintegration. Feminism helped split apart God's order, first of marriage, then of sex and children.

Girl: "Living Together Is as Good as Marriage." "We don't need a piece of paper to keep us together," a young couple said to me in the early 1970s. Back then, not getting married was a radical notion; but with divorce rates climbing, many social scientists thought living together would be the perfect solution. Couples could have the experience of marriage without the legalities. Then, if it didn't work out, each just agreed to go separate ways. And, researchers thought, if the couples did marry, they would be more likely to stay together.

Now cohabitation is mainstream. In fact, it is more common for couples today to move in together than to marry first. Yet, cohabiting couples do not go on to stronger marriages; their divorce rate is higher than for couples who did not live together before marriage.

Girl: "I Don't Have to Be Married to Have Children." Illegitimate birth rates have soared since the 1960s. But there is more to this phenomenon than raw numbers; it reflects a change of attitude. Bearing illegitimate children used to be shameful. Now, 55 percent of teenage girls say they would consider having a child out of wedlock.[7] Sports and entertainment celebrities grace the pages of newspapers and magazines with announcements that the couple is expecting a baby—"but they have no plans to marry," the articles say. And ordinary folk are following their example.

Teenage sexual activity and teen pregnancy rates dropped between 1991 and 1996, but this is not entirely good news. In 1980 most teens who gave birth were married. That is not true today: two-thirds of Hispanic and white teen mothers are unmarried, and 95 percent of black teen mothers are unmarried.[8] Perhaps the single most harmful message our daughters are hearing is that marriage, sex, and children need not go together.

Application *Teach your daughter the seventh commandment and the answer to question 96 of the Catechism for Young Children: "What does the seventh commandment teach you? Not to have sex with anyone outside the bonds of holy marriage."[9]*

Peer Pressure

Having friends who smoke will influence your daughter more than cigarette commercials. The popular girls in junior high will influence her more than a pop music star. The way the girls in her group interact with boys will influence her more than the movies she sees. Her peers have a louder, more immediate voice than movies, songs, or commercials.

Because the most influential group is her friends, keep a close watch on her friends and the way they handle the changes of puberty. I've called it the "middle school syndrome" because just about the time they enter middle school, girls begin to change, and not all of it for the better. They start to wear clothes their parents didn't (and wouldn't!) pick out for them. They show real interest in *boys*. They pick their own radio stations. They go into their rooms, close the door, and don't come out for hours. Even knowing this, we weren't prepared for Ellie to announce that her friend down the street was "looking forward to the day when she could . . . you know, Mom."

Peer pressure is powerful. People want to be liked. Teenage girls want to be popular. Those who put popularity first will do what they know is wrong, dangerous, bad for them, or just plain stupid in order to fit in.

Imagine that the boy your daughter likes asks her out, takes her to a party, and offers her a drink. Will she blow her chance with the boy or take the drink? Will she, in front of her friends, call you to come and pick her up?

In a situation like this, making the right choice will take strength and conviction. It will take good judgment and wisdom and the fear of God. Good judgment will enable her to see that the boy she likes isn't worth it. Strength and conviction will help her stand up to her peers' taunts. Wisdom will remind her that breaking God's commands leads to trouble. "To fear the LORD is to hate evil" (Prov. 8:13). To fear the Lord is to know that there are consequences to sin.

Application *Ask your daughter what ideas are popular with her friends and schoolmates. Help her judge whether these ideas follow what the Bible says we should do. Talk with her about making the right choice even if it makes her unpopular.*

Saplings in a Storm?

Clinical psychologist Mary Pipher compares young teenage girls to "saplings in a storm." They are "young and vulnerable trees that the winds blow with gale strength." Their own developmental changes, the broader American culture, and the expectation that they should distance themselves from their parents hit them in junior high like a "hurricane." But the storm dies down in their later high school years. Then, like saplings that spring back after the winds, they regain their "selves," their self-confidence, their self-esteem. There is no lasting damage. As long as they turn out to be interesting adults, it doesn't matter terribly much what they did as teens.[10] No harm, no foul.

Not true. Solomon warned his son not to give his best years to practicing sin, because someday he would regret the things he did: "At the end of your life you will groan. . . . You will say, 'How I hated discipline! How my heart spurned correction!' " (Prov. 5:11–12). Teach your daughter that what she does matters, and warn her that sin always has harmful consequences.

But don't expect her to be perfect. She is a sinner. She is young, and very often she will be foolish. She will make mistakes, and at times she will be openly defiant. Even the best daughter will sometimes do something stupid, maybe even dangerous or self-destructive. Remember that she needs to grow in grace and wisdom, and that won't happen all at once. Be patient, gentle, and compassionate. Remind her over and over that God is ever ready to forgive and help his children. Show her what God's love is like by always being ready to forgive her and help her when she loses her temper, leaves the kitchen a mess, does something foolish, or otherwise shows you that she is not perfect.

Don't expect to be the perfect parent. You will not always be patient and wise; at times you will lose your temper or make wrong decisions. Even if you are an experienced parent, you are still growing in grace and wisdom. You won't always have the answers.

By confessing your own failures to her and to God, you teach your daughter to confess hers as well. Teach her that God forgives repentant sinners of all their sins (1 John 1:9), but he is not indifferent about whether she sins (see Rom. 6:1–18). Remind her that God wants her to be holy (1 Peter 1:13–16).

Application *In family devotions read Romans 5:6–8:39. Ask, How can we be forgiven for our sins? Does it matter if we keep on sinning? Will we keep on sinning? What does it mean to die with Christ? To live by the Spirit? Can anything separate us from God's love? Does that mean we can do anything we want? Have your daughter memorize 1 Peter 1:15b–16: "So be holy in all you do; for it is written: 'Be holy, because I am holy.' "*

"Get Wisdom"

Sonya grew up in a series of foster homes. At thirteen, she married an older man. She didn't know it, but he already had a wife and five children. Soon she had two children of her own, and then her "husband" deserted her. Sonya was poor and poorly educated; she could barely read. She had to earn a living and rear two boys in the inner city by herself. When her younger son was fourteen, he pulled a knife on a classmate. Sounds like another urban tragedy. But it wasn't.

Sonya's sons have grown up now. Her older son is an engineer married to a doctor; they have two daughters. Her younger son, the one who pulled out the knife, is the director of pediatric neurosurgery at Johns Hopkins Hospital; he and his wife have three sons. How could a poor, single mother in Baltimore overcome such odds?

After the knife incident, she realized that she had to protect her children from the bad influences all around them. She made her boys come home, do homework, and read. What they read made a difference. "Both of my boys could read much better than I could. . . . So I had them read me my favorite book—the book of Proverbs. Then I asked them to explain to me what they had read."[11]

This extraordinary story is a model for us parents of daughters. As Sonya and her sons meditated in the Word, God protected them from the bad influences around them and brought the boys safely through the teenage years to a useful adulthood. They became men of righteousness, wisdom, and good character. Our daughters need the same working of God's grace.

The world is waiting to fill our daughters' minds with lies. The chapters that follow will help you turn down the world's noise and expose your daughter to God's grace by training her in righteousness and wisdom and by teaching her what she needs to know about herself, good character, sex, dating, and marriage.

Although the storm our daughters face may seem fiercer than in years past, it consists of the same elements God's people have always faced: the world and our own sin nature. That means our hope is still in God and his Word. And what we teach our daughters is what good parents have always taught their sons and daughters: "wisdom, discipline, and understanding" (Prov. 23:23).

For Further Thought and Discussion

1. Read Matthew 5:13–16; Romans 12:1–2; and 1 John 2:15–17. Define "world" as it is used in these verses.

How does this world influence us? How do you see it influencing your daughter? How should a Christian relate to this world?

2. Read Romans 1:18–32; 12:1–2; 1 Corinthians 2:14–16; and Colossians 3:1–17. How does what we think influence what we do? How are we renewed in mind? As our minds are renewed, how do we change?

3. Read Proverbs 5:1–23 and Hebrews 11:25. How do the cords of sin hold us fast? Why is it so easy to give one's early (best) years to sin? What do you want your daughter to look back on in twenty years?

4. Read Psalm 119. Why should we judge everything by God's Word? How does God's Word keep our way pure? How can you encourage your daughter to use the Scriptures to keep her way pure?

5. Read Matthew 5:48; Romans 3:10–24; 4:1–8; 5:6–11; Philippians 3:7–9; and 1 Peter 1:16. Who meets God's standard of perfection? Can we earn God's love and favor? How can sinners be holy and perfect? Why would the expectation that she always be perfect crush your daughter's spirit? How would knowing that she is a forgiven sinner give your daughter freedom, power over sin, joy, and hope?

6. Read Psalm 103:1–18. How does God treat believers when we sin? Why does he treat us this way? How, then, should parents treat their own children?

7. Read Proverbs 23:12–26. How can your daughter get wisdom, discipline, and understanding? What must you do? What must she do?

PART 2

The Right Foundation

Point for Prayer

 Pray that you would set a good example for your daughter by living a life worthy of the Lord.

○ ○ ○

"Follow my example, as I follow the example of Christ." —1 Corinthians 11:1

CHAPTER 3

Show Her the Right Way

"I'm becoming more like my mother/father every day!" is the lament of baby boomers in middle age. How many times do you catch yourself saying or doing something you vowed as a teenager you would never say or do to your own children? Yet, we grow up to be more like our parents than we ever intended.

Teenagers want to be different from their parents, and they try to prove they are by the clothes they wear, the hairstyles they adopt, the language they use, the music they listen to, and the activities they pursue—and by never being seen in public with their parents. And yet, they also become like their parents. This is both good and bad.

Sin Trickles Down

Water flowed through a series of bowls suspended over our heads as we walked through the flower show display. A small bowl overflowed into a larger one directly below it. Other bowls were connected by bamboo pipes. Sometimes the water's path was hard to trace, but at the lowest point of the artificial stream, the water was pumped back to the top, recycled in a continuous loop.

Like this water, sin "recycles" through families. Sin follows the trickle down theory: What starts at the top (parents) "trickles down" to the bottom (children). That is the nature of sin and of people.

Children suffer the consequences of their parents' sins because some sins have natural consequences: the sluggard will not provide for his family (Prov. 6:9–11); "a greedy man brings trouble to his family" (15:27); a drunkard "will come to poverty" (23:21 NASB; see also 21:17); a foolish woman tears her house down with her own hands (14:1). Children are caught in the path of their parents' sin. Other sins are "transmitted" from parent to child.

Children Imitate Their Parents

Karen didn't like her daughter's boyfriend. He reminded her too much of her ex-husband. "Why can't she see that he's just like her father?" she asked. "He's irresponsible, he drinks, and I think he hits her. Why does she have to make the same mistake I made?"

Abused children abuse their own children, generation after generation. Scientists are searching for an "alcoholism gene." Children born out of wedlock are more likely to have out-of-wedlock children themselves. Children keep repeating their parents' mistakes.

Children Live Up to Our Expectations

A teacher in a rural school district had a parent conference with the mother of a girl who was not doing well in her classes and not turning in her homework. The mother said, "Well, they never could learn me nothin' either." The girl was not only imitating her mother's bad school habits; she was also fulfilling her mother's expectations.

Parents who expect their children to use drugs and schools that give out condoms because they expect teenagers to have sex think they are just being "realistic." But such expectations tend to *shape* reality—rather than reflect it—by treating these behaviors as inevitable.

Children Are Born to Sin

Children are born ready to imitate their parents' bad habits because they are born sinners (see Gen. 6:5; Ps. 51:5). Every one of us is "born with a depraved and corrupt nature. And this inner corruption is the unholy fountain of all actual sins."[1] This is why we have bad habits for our children to imitate. This is why children easily imitate the bad we do, but we have to work hard to get our children to imitate the good.

Righteousness Rains Down

Sin recycles through families "to the third and fourth generation," but righteousness blesses a "thousand generations" or "to the most extended generation possible"[2] (Deut. 5:9–10; see also 6:1–3; Ps. 103:17–18). Children suffer the consequences of their parents' sin, but they also reap the blessings from their parents' obedience. "The righteous man leads a blameless life; blessed are his children after him" (Prov. 20:7).

When you sow righteousness and seek the Lord, he showers you and your children with righteousness and unfailing love (Hos. 10:12; see also Isa. 44:1–5) and starts a new cycle of blessing. As a flood overcomes a trickle, so his blessings override the curses of sin.

You Are an Example for Your Daughter

"Who taught you to use drugs?" an angry father demands of his son. "You!" shouts the son. The voice-over says, "Parents who use drugs have children who use drugs." This public service advertisement reminded us that children learn more from what we do than from what we say. We are always teaching our daughters simply by living.

So then, we must be careful to "live a life worthy of the Lord . . . bearing fruit in every good work" (Col. 1:10). We should be humble, gentle, and patient; speak the truth in love; put off falsehood; not steal, but work with our hands; have no bitterness, anger, or rage; not engage in unwholesome talk, foolish talk, obscenity, or coarse joking; not engage in drunkenness or debauchery; not display greed; not brawl or slander others; have no hint of sexual immorality or impurity; forgive one another; be characterized by thanksgiving; look after orphans and widows; not show favoritism; be peacemakers; "walk as Jesus did" (Eph. 4:2–5:21; 1 Thess. 4:3–12; James 1:19–3:18; 1 John 2:6).

Live the Ten Commandments

One day I took Ellie shopping. The store was crowded, and we stood in the checkout line a long time before our several purchases were rung up. As we walked out, I checked the receipt, because I had figured in my head a larger total than we paid. Perhaps something was on sale—but no, the clerk had missed a $10 item. The line was still long, and no one in the store would have known the clerk hadn't rung up that item. It would have been easier and faster just to shrug my shoulders and go home. But I would have missed an opportunity to teach Ellie what it means to obey the eighth commandment. So, we went back, stood in line again, and called the mistake to the clerk's attention.

You can show your daughter how to obey the Ten Commandments by living out their meaning. When she sees you honor your own parents, she learns to respect and obey you. If you joyfully and faithfully attend Sunday worship, she learns to keep the Sabbath. Do you gossip about your neighbors or use racial slurs? If so, you teach your daughter to disobey the ninth commandment.

Does your daughter see you forgiving others or holding grudges (Matt. 18:21–22; Mark 11:25; Luke 17:3–4)? Does she see you nursing small wrongs or letting love cover a multitude of sins (Prov. 10:12; 1 Cor. 13:5; 1 Peter 4:8)? Do you collect material wealth for your own comfort but neglect to lay up treasures in heaven (Matt. 6:19–21)? Or do you give to the church, to missions, to the poor?

My parents have a huge vegetable garden every summer. They always grow much more than they could ever use and then offer vegetables to anyone who needs them. Their practice is a very tangible example of generosity and cheerful giving. When you obey Jesus' commands, you set a good example for your daughter to follow.

Application *Read Deuteronomy 5–6 in family devotions. Ask, Why did God give the Ten Commandments? Is it good to keep the commandments today? How do we keep them today? Have your daughter memorize the Ten Commandments.*

Show Your Daughter What a Woman Is

When Ellie was in fifth grade, my husband took her to his client's office on Take Your Daughter to Work Day, but she learns much more about what a woman can do by how her father talks about women when he is at home than she did by tagging along for a few hours at work. She learns what a woman is by what her parents do and how we treat each other and her every day.

Through Your Marriage. I once counseled a woman whose husband watched pornographic videos and kept pornographic magazines in his closet. His habit affected not only their marriage but also his daughters. After his wife persuaded him to get counseling, he repented, threw out all his pornography, and started leading his family in nightly devotions. Now his daughters see their mother and father treating each other with respect and kindness. They have a better example of what a woman is.

One of the best things you can do for your daughter is have a good marriage, one in which husband and wife love, help, and respect one another. This is true not just because children in two-parent families have a higher standard of living, do better in school, are less likely to be abused, and have fewer social problems. A good marriage shows a girl what a woman should be—her mother by what she does and her father by how he treats his wife.

When a girl sees her mother, like the excellent wife of Proverbs 31, loving and doing good to her father, working hard and helping him with family and community responsibilities, fearing God and helping her neighbors, and giving her whole heart to the tasks God has given her to do, she learns that a woman is able to influence her home and community, make good use of the gifts God has given her, and serve God and help others. When she sees her father loving and respecting her mother, valuing her contributions, and appreciating her abilities, she has a good picture of what a woman is.

Through Your Affection. A popular bumper sticker asked, "Have you hugged your child today?" Not only does your daughter need to see her parents hugging each other; she needs both parents to hug *her,* especially after she reaches puberty.[3] In fact, it seems that a father's affection is crucial to girls. A study of girls without a father in the home found that many "were overly responsive to males and displayed early and inappropriate sexual behavior," and they were much more likely to have a premarital birth.[4] For all their seeming independence, teenage girls don't really want to be cut loose from their parents. Their parents' affection helps them feel secure at a time when everything else is changing.

Parents who hug their daughters also help them learn how to express affection appropriately. They learn that love doesn't have to be sexual; it can be shown by a quick squeeze of the hand or a touch on the shoulder. A girl who experiences her parents' affection isn't "starving for love," looking for someone—finally—to love her. Pregnant teenage girls commonly say that they want to keep their babies because then "I'll have someone to love me" or "I'll have someone to love." Make sure your daughter already has someone to love and to love her—you!

Application *Hug your daughter. Sit close to her on the sofa, or hold her on your lap. Brush her hair. Have a water balloon fight or a water pistol shoot-out. Remember: she is never too old for affection.*

Through Your Expectations. In our household of three daughters, we have a saying: "You get no points for being helpless." You teach your daughter what a woman is by what you expect of her. She knows what you expect by how you treat her, how you talk to her, and what she does that you get excited about. One high school football coach said that he would rather his daughter have a steady boyfriend than make the honor roll. He was teaching his daughter that popularity is the most important thing.

Your daughter first learns to see herself through you. The way you live, the kind of person you are, is an example to your daughter, but you must be more than a silent example.

Roy wanted to be a good witness to his neighbors. When his neighbor's car got stuck in the snow, Roy was there with his tractor to help pull it out. When the neighbor's tree was hit by lightning, Roy was there with a chain saw to help take it down. Over the years, Roy was always helpful, always friendly, but he never could bring himself to raise the subject of the gospel.

One day, after yet another good deed, his neighbor hemmed and hawed, and Roy wondered if this would be his big chance to talk to his neighbor about his faith in Christ. The neighbor finally got up his courage, looked Roy in the eye, and asked, "Roy—are you a vegetarian?"

Like Roy, you could live an exemplary life, and your daughter could come to the wrong conclusions. You must also train her in the way she should go (Prov. 22:6) by bringing her up in the training and instruction *of the Lord* (Eph. 6:4).

For Further Thought and Discussion

1. Read Deuteronomy 5:8–10. In what ways do the sins of the parents affect their children? In what ways does God bless the children of believers? Why do you think God links blessing families to the second commandment? Do you need to break a cycle of sin in your family?

2. Read Deuteronomy 6:1–9; Psalm 103; and Isaiah 44:1–5. What promises do you find for you and your daughter? What responsibilities do you find for parents?

3. Read Ephesians 6:1–3. Then read Proverbs 1:8–9; 3:1–2; 5:1–2; 6:20–24. Why does the fifth commandment also hold a promise for children who honor their parents? What are the benefits to children who obey their parents in the Lord?

4. Read Ephesians 3:14–6:20; Colossians 1:9–14; 1 Thessalonians 4:3–12; and James 1:19–3:18. List the behaviors that are worthy of the Lord and our high calling. Which of these are you demonstrating to your daughter? Which are you not? How can you walk more worthily of the Lord?

Points for Prayer

❧ Pray for wisdom to set reasonable rules and enforce them.

❧ Pray that your daughter would have a teachable and tender heart.

"He who spares the rod hates his son, but he who loves him is careful to discipline him." —Proverbs 13:24

CHAPTER 4

Take Time to Discipline

Espalier is a fruit tree trained to grow flat onto a trellis or against a wall. It looks like a cute new way to grow a tree, but professional growers do it because it exposes all the branches to sunlight and allows the tree to produce more fruit. However, it takes extra work. The gardener doesn't just plant the tree against a wall or frame and expect it to grow into the proper shape. After all, trees don't naturally grow onto walls with their branches equally spaced like candelabra.

The grower considers the shape he wants. He provides the frame or wall onto which the tree will grow. He watches the direction in which the branches are growing and prunes or redirects them when they begin to go the wrong way. He fastens branches to the wall or frame to hold them in place as they grow. The result of all his diligent labor is a greater harvest of fruit.

To see the fruit of the Spirit in your daughter, you must be actively disciplining, pruning, fastening, and directing her in the way she should go. Just as trees don't naturally grow to look like candelabra, children don't naturally grow to be godly. It takes the work of the Holy Spirit and the everyday involvement of parents to train a daughter in the disciplines of the Lord.

Discipline, Don't Exasperate

"Do not provoke your children to anger; but bring them up in the discipline and instruction of the Lord" (Eph. 6:4 NASB). This may seem contradictory; after all, discipline is not usually pleasant (Heb. 12:11), and children often get angry when parents say no. The proof of good discipline is not whether your daughter ever loses her temper under it, but whether she is being trained in righteousness. Is she continually frustrated, growing bitter, and feeling humiliated and discouraged (Col. 3:21) or learning to love and respect God and her parents (Heb. 12:9a)? Godly discipline does not add fuel to the fire of her sinful anger but guides her into righteousness. By its very nature, discipline will sometimes infuriate your daughter. But reasonable rules, appropriate punishments, praise, and the dynamics of forgiveness will help keep your discipline from exasperating her unnecessarily.

Set Reasonable Rules

Pick a few basic rules appropriate to your daughter's age, situation, and spiritual maturity. Then enforce them consistently. Think about what you are willing to hold to each and every time. You will be fighting against your daughter's strong will, pleading, and wheedling and against your own fatigue and reluctance to make her unhappy. If you punish her for something one time and let her get away with it the next, she will be tempted to see if she can get away with it *this* time, she will feel mistreated and resentful when she is punished, and your discipline will be ineffective.

Ask yourself, *Is there something here contrary to Scripture, or is this just a matter of my taste?* What if she does color her hair with Jell-O or wear a necklace chain around her waist, a toe ring, and six earrings in each ear? It may look strange, but is it sinful? Does it reflect an attitude you don't want her to develop? Should you raise your tolerance threshold for teenage fashions or draw the proverbial line in the sand?

Use Appropriate Punishments

One of our daughter's friends was routinely grounded for a month. We used to wonder what the parents did if, while she was already grounded, she did something else that required discipline. She could have been under perpetual house arrest!

Think of how you can best get your daughter's attention and how you can tie the punishment to the crime in a way that teaches her godliness. Appropriate discipline shows her the seriousness of what she has done, protects her from bad influences and costly mistakes, and gives her the structure she needs to do what is right. Use punishments that teach your daughter self-discipline and respect for others. Remember that your goal is to train your daughter to do what is right (Prov. 19:18; 23:13–16; 29:17). Remember that God corrects his children with gentleness and love, and so treat your daughter with gentleness, love, and respect when you correct her.

Don't forget to teach her to confess her sins to God and receive his forgiveness. You can help her understand God's forgiveness by the way you correct her. Be careful not to hold her failures over her head or bring them up time after time. Discipline her, assure her of your love and support, and then treat her as if you have forgotten her sin. Pray that she would experience the joy of knowing she is forgiven.

Application *If you don't already have established rules and punishments for your daughter, make them and tell her what they are. Then enforce them with loving firmness.*

Remember to Praise

In third grade, Ellie had to make a costume and present a report on a country for social studies. We worked on the costume for over a month. She got brochures and interviewed people who had traveled or stayed in the country. She had photographs, native crafts, and songs in the native language. When she came home on presentation day, I asked her how the teacher liked it. "She didn't say anything," Ellie replied. "What about the other reports?" I asked. "She didn't say anything about anybody's report," Ellie answered.

Sometime later a newsletter came from school in which the teacher mentioned what a good job the students had done, but she never told the students themselves. This teacher was quick to punish her class, but she never praised them. By the end of the school year, the students were frustrated and no longer motivated to do their best work. You can frustrate your daughter if your communication to her is characterized by punishment, criticism, and disappointment, but she will thrive under praise.

One summer I worked as a camp counselor. We were told to "ignore bad behavior and reward good behavior." It became one of our favorite jokes, because one cannot deal effectively with children only by praising them. Children need both correction and praise, reproof and training in righteousness.

Our heavenly Father is the model parent. Through the Scriptures, he both teaches (positive) and rebukes (negative), corrects (negative) and trains (positive) "so that the man of God may be thoroughly equipped for every good work" (2 Tim. 3:16–17). God does not shrink from inflicting painful discipline (Heb. 12:4–11). But he also blesses (Ps. 5:12; Eph. 1:3), comforts (Isa. 51:12; 2 Cor. 1:3–5; 7:6), and encourages us (Acts 9:31; Rom. 15:5). He comes alongside us (Matt. 28:20; John 14:16–18; Heb. 13:5) and carries us tenderly (Isa. 40:11). He understands our weakness (Isa. 42:3; Heb. 4:14–16). "The LORD has compassion on those who fear him; for he knows how we are formed, he remembers that we are dust" (Ps. 103:13–14). He always forgives and welcomes his repentant children (Luke 15:11–24; 1 John 1:9). We must treat our children with both discipline and compassion, as the Lord deals with us.

Ask for Forgiveness

When I asked a class of young children, "Do parents sin?" most of them answered, "No!" Older children don't harbor such illusions. Not exasperating your daughter means admitting to her when you make mistakes or sin against her. Confession of failures and faults is not weakness but godly humility. You are treating her as Scripture says we should treat anyone of the household of faith (Matt. 5:23–24; 7:3–5; see also Prov. 28:13).

Her feelings may be hurt more easily than you realize. Remember that teenage girls "reason emotionally," and it takes very little to make them feel unloved and unlovable. Girls are likely to say, "My father doesn't love me," because he just yelled at her.

When you make a practice of asking your daughter's forgiveness whenever you sin against her, several good things happen:

- You teach her that everyone needs Jesus.
- You teach her how to ask forgiveness of others.
- You teach her to forgive those who hurt her.
- You teach her to trust and respect you.

As part of my graduate studies, I observed counseling sessions with families. Invariably, the first assignment was to make lists of sins committed against one another and ask for forgiveness. The changes by the following week were dramatic. What had seemed insurmountable problems and irreconcilable differences virtually disappeared through the simple action of asking for and giving forgiveness. All the changes these families made in subsequent weeks were based on this first exercise. You need not wait for a family crisis to ask forgiveness of your daughter. Go to her whenever you become aware of any wrong you have done her.

Application *Do you need to ask your daughter's forgiveness for a sin against her? Do it today.*

What If She Doesn't Think Your Rules Are **Reasonable?**

The teenager who thinks all her parents' rules are reasonable doesn't exist. Even the best-taught daughter will rebel from time to time. She is, after all, still a sinner. Some daughters just seem to have a stronger will and a greater talent for rebellion. They question every rule and resent correction. What *can* you do when she says, "No; I won't!"?

Have the right attitude. Expect her to obey. Remember that she does not have your experience or perspective, and that children don't always know their own best interests. Be loving but firm. Stay calm. Don't argue. Don't shout. You won't persuade her simply by being louder. Anger is often a sign that you don't feel confident that you're doing the right thing.

Talk to her. Tell her you love her. Explain that God has given you the responsibility to look out for her and to train her to do the right things. Tell her you would never get over it if you let something really bad happen to her.

Listen to her side. Be willing to negotiate some of the rules some of the time, but don't compromise on her safety. You wouldn't debate whether or not she may run out into the street in front of a car. Don't negotiate if you think it is really unsafe or sinful.

Ask for her forgiveness. Maybe you were the one who was wrong. If you have made mistakes in the past that you are now correcting, ask her to forgive you for not being the parent God expected you to be.

Make sure disobedience carries consequences. Tell her that she can choose to disobey, but spell out the specific consequences if she does. Then carry out those consequences consistently.

Be willing to accept "half a loaf." Reward her steps toward obedience. Your daughter isn't perfect. Remember that God graciously accepts *our* imperfect obedience.

Pray that God would make you wise. Pray that he would show you when you are being unreasonable and strengthen your conviction when you are being wise.

Pray that God would change your daughter's heart to listen to advice and accept correction.

The older your daughter becomes, the less control you will have over her. You won't be able to compel her to do everything you want, but you always have the duty before God to do what is right. When you set reasonable limits and rules, and then discipline her lovingly and consistently, you are doing what is right. A parent who doesn't discipline a child hates her (Prov. 13:24) and is a "willing party to [her] death" (19:18), that is, the death of her soul (23:13–14). Think of that when you set rules or say no. It will put your daughter's temper tantrum in perspective.

Keep at It

One spring I was too busy to do much gardening. *It won't matter,* I thought. *I liked the way everything looked last summer. The plants are mature enough now that the gardens shouldn't need work anyway.* I had forgotten that gardens are never finished; they are always growing and changing. In July, as I worked to restore order in the garden, I thought, *If only I had gotten to this sooner, I wouldn't have nearly this much work to do!*

Like gardens, children are also growing, changing, and maturing. They reach an age at which they are old enough to do most things for themselves, they are enthusiastic about everything, they play happily with their neighborhood friends, and they think Mom and Dad are wonderful and wise. Parents think they can sit back and relax now. The hard work is done; their children will continue just as they are—practically perfect. But, like inexperienced or lazy gardeners, soon they will wonder what happened to their happy, cooperative little girls.

The weeds of bad habits seem to get extra fertilizer when girls hit puberty. Huge behavior problems spring up unexpectedly. She develops an "attitude." She cares more about what her friends think than about what you think. She can be cynical, rude, and selfish. Now is the time to be as attentive as you were during her preschool years. Though she is much bigger now, she resembles a toddler more than she would be flattered to think.

You won't instill instant godliness. Children need to hear the same lessons over and over, and in different contexts; and they need practice applying them to actual situations. Because she is young, your daughter doesn't have your mental or emotional maturity; she doesn't reason the same way you do; she doesn't see nuances, draw analogies, or make connections that seem obvious to you. She needs time to grow and mature.

She also needs to spend time with *you.* Today's families are busier than ever. We don't eat meals together, both parents work outside the home, and the pace of modern life has each of us going in a different direction. Parents have less time with their children and less energy when they are together. Make time to be with your daughter, at home and away from home, at night and in the morning, as you go about your daily tasks (Deut. 6:6–9). When you spend time with her, she sees your faith in action, and you get natural opportunities to talk to her and train her in practical Christian living.

Pray

While we can train, correct, and direct our daughters, they are not like fruit trees or gardens in every way. We can't completely prune away bad habits or make good habits flourish. Only God can grow a godly daughter. Our daughters will grow into godly women as they are united to and abiding in Christ (John 15:1–17).

Because we must rely on God to make our training and discipline truly effective, we parents must pray. Some daughters seem to obey their parents immediately, but with others it is always a battle. Some daughters feel drawn to a particular kind of work at a young age; others graduate from college still wondering what future God has for them. Some daughters come to faith in Jesus before you might even think they're old enough to understand, while others don't seem at all close to faith. Your prayers should be specific to your daughter and her situation, but keep these broad categories in mind as you pray for her:

- her relationship with God
- her relationships with others
- growth in wisdom, good character, and the fruit of the Spirit
- strength against temptation and to make a good witness before her peers
- joy and satisfaction in serving God
- guidance for her future

Above all, pray that God would extend his grace to her and that she would learn to rely on him.

Discipline Is More Than Punishment

The first thing we think of when we see "discipline" and "children" in the same sentence is punishment. But discipline is much more than that. Discipline is training that corrects, molds, and perfects moral character. One tool for teaching discipline is punishment and correction, but discipline also includes instruction and practice. A student and an athlete are "disciplined"— their abilities are drawn out and developed— by sound teaching and appropriate exercises.

The Bible tells us parents to bring our children up in the "discipline" and instruction of the Lord (Eph. 6:4 NASB). As you teach your daughter the discipline of godly habits—such as reading her Bible and showing mercy to others—it will deepen her relationship with God.

For Further Thought and Discussion

1. Read Deuteronomy 6:1–9 and Ephesians 6:4. What should we be teaching our daughters? What does God want them to know and do?

2. Read Ephesians 6:4 and Colossians 3:21. How can we discourage, exasperate, and embitter our daughters? How can we encourage them?

3. Read Luke 15:11–24; John 14:16–18; 2 Corinthians 1:3–5; 2 Timothy 3:16–17; and Hebrews 12:4–11. How does God the Father treat his children? How can you follow his example?

4. Read Proverbs 13:24; 15:32; 19:8, 18; 22:6, 15; 23:13–16, 24–26a; 29:15, 17; and Hebrews 12:1–13. What is discipline? What are the benefits of discipline? Why is discipline proof of love? What happens when parents do not discipline a child? Why is there hope in discipline? Why must discipline involve more than punishment? Are you disciplining your daughter in such a way as to "save her soul from death"? If not, how can you begin to?

Point for Prayer

🐾 Pray that your daughter would grow in good character and good works.

"Train a child in the way he should go, and when he is old
he will not turn from it." —Proverbs 22:6

C H A P T E R   5

Instill the Right Habits

Our first house was heated by a coal furnace. One chilly fall morning, John went down to start the first fire of the season. Soon the house was filled with smoke—the chimney was blocked. While John called the chimney sweep, I opened all the windows to let in fresh air. It was some time before the smoke cleared enough to close the windows, and months later we could still smell smoke in the attic closets.

Instilling godly habits in your daughter is like airing out a house.[1] Good habits will gradually replace bad ones just as air from outside gradually replaces the air inside a house. New habits don't develop overnight. You are instilling in your daughter something contrary to her nature—godliness—and that will take time.

Sanctification, or growing to be more like Jesus, growing in godliness and holiness, involves more than putting off the sin nature, the "old self." Its positive side is putting on the "new self" (Eph. 4:22–24; Col. 3:9–10). Bringing up your daughter to love and obey the Lord means more than correcting her when she does wrong. You not only prune away bad habits but also instill godly habits.

God is the one who sanctifies your daughter. If she believes in Jesus, he has begun a good work in her that he *will* complete

(Rom. 8:29–30; Phil. 1:6). He will raise her up when she stumbles, guide her back when she strays, and renew her in heart, mind, and actions. He will make her more and more like Jesus, but he uses you to do that. Through the work of the Holy Spirit in her heart and in yours, you can help your daughter develop the habits that foster greater love for and obedience to God.

How do you teach your daughter to pray, to read the Bible regularly, to visit the sick, and to show patience? You do it by providing the right environment for these practices to grow into habits.

Get Her Reading the Bible

God's grace comes through his Word. It is living and active (Heb. 4:12), God-breathed and useful (2 Tim. 3:16), and God works his purposes through it (Isa. 55:11). There, your daughter learns what Jesus has done. The Holy Spirit uses the Scriptures to change her and to nurture the fruit of the Spirit. God's Word brings her wisdom and understanding (Ps. 119:98–100), comfort (v. 52), joy (v. 111), peace (v. 165), hope (v. 116), and strength to resist sin (v. 11). Through it, God communes with her, and she learns about his promises, his faithfulness, and his lovingkindness.

Application *Teach your daughter how to keep an "interactive journal." The older she is, the more she can include in her journal.*

Pen it: *Write out Scripture passages word for word in a notebook.*

Ponder it: *Ask Who? What? When? Where? How? Why? What does this word mean? Is this a command? A promise? What does it tell me about Jesus? God? The Holy Spirit? Teach her how to look up cross references, do a word study, find historical or geographical information, or use a commentary. As she finds answers or notices something, have her write it down in her notebook.*

Personalize it: *Find principles that apply to her.*

Perform it: *Think of specific ways to apply those principles in her life.*[2]

Teach Her to Apply the Bible

As often as you can, give her scriptural reasons for what you want her to do. This may be as simple as "Because the fifth commandment says you should obey your parents," but as she grows older, she will appreciate and respond to more thoughtful answers.

"Why can't I wear this skirt to school? All the kids are wearing them." "You're not leaving the house dressed like that!" is not the most helpful answer, either for your relationship with your daughter or for her relationship with God. If, on the other hand, you help her to understand that God expects her to avoid the appearance of evil and not to lead another to stumble into sin, and that her body is a temple of the Holy Spirit, she will learn a practical way to obey God and will likely be more cooperative as well. She will begin to see that God's commandments deal with ordinary, everyday decisions. (For more on applying God's Word to everyday life, see pages 102–4.)

Start a Bible Memory Program

Years ago, I met a Christian who had been a prisoner of war in Vietnam. The Vietnamese did not treat their prisoners according to the rules of the Geneva Convention. Any Bibles (or other personal items) the prisoners had were taken away, and they were denied the most basic of comforts. Together, the prisoners wrote down all the Bible verses they could remember on scraps of paper and hid them from the guards. Eventually they had significant portions of Scripture written down, and they read them daily. Those verses became a lifeline to faith, peace, and comfort in the midst of extreme hardship.

We hope our daughters will never suffer as these men did, but God's Word hidden in their hearts will come to them when they need it and keep them through temptation, trial, and triumph.

Pray with Her

Children trust God with a simplicity that often puts our so-phisticated reasoning to shame. They expect God to answer. Yet, children also need to learn how to pray. When I invite my Sunday school class to pray, most of the children are embar-rassed and reluctant to pray aloud. They don't know what to say. However, if I pray first, they will pray after, often using the same prayer or praying for the same things I did. Eventually, they learn to pray in their own words and for their own re-quests. Children learn to pray as we pray with them.

When you pray with your daughter, you teach her how to talk to God and what to ask him to do. You let her look into your own heart and see that you want to know Jesus better and you want her to know Jesus better. Children follow our exam-ple and live up to our expectations. By praying with her, you set a good example and show her what you hope, by God's grace, she will become. Most important, when you pray with your daughter, you are seeking God's grace in her life and in yours.

Ask her what *she* wants to pray about. That will tell you a lot about the state of her heart. You will see whether she is learn-ing to confess her sins and thank God for his forgiveness, whether she is looking to God for strength to resist temptation, whether she wants to give a good witness before her peers, whether she is learning to love her neighbor, what she is strug-gling with, and what she understands about the Bible. You can add what she prays for (or doesn't pray for) to your list of prayers for her.

Take Her to Church

Sunday worship is part of the structure your daughter needs. There she learns to keep the Sabbath, and she partici-pates in things that help her grow in faith: prayer, Bible read-ing and teaching, and fellowship with God and with other

Christians. In church, she encounters the Word and prayer in ways she cannot in private or family devotions, and she is exposed to the gospel in the signs of baptism and the Lord's Supper. When your daughter learns to love church, she builds another habit of godliness (see Deut. 5:12–15; Heb. 10:25).

She also develops relationships with the other members of the church. She gets to know adults who can advise her, teach her, watch over her, and pray for her. She makes friends with others her own age who are growing up in Christian homes and who can stand up with her to do what is right. Girls who have close relationships with other adults and with friends who share the right values are more likely to stay out of trouble.

Application *Get to know your daughter's Sunday school teacher. Is the teacher clearly explaining the gospel and the Scriptures to her? Does the teacher see evidence of godly character growing in her? What questions does she ask the teacher? What does she seem not to understand? Mention things the teacher can pray about for your daughter.*

Ground Her in the Faith

"Spring" starts early at our house, in February, when the seed packets arrive in the mail. I sow seeds in trays and count the days until they sprout. When the seedlings have only a few leaves, I have to plant them in deeper containers, because the trays are too shallow for the roots to grow. If I didn't put them in deeper soil, the plants would soon die.

Jesus told a parable about seed. Some fell on shallow, rocky soil. That seed sprouted quickly because it lay on top of the soil, but the plant that grew also died quickly because it had developed no roots (Mark 4:3–6). The seed is the Word of God, and the plants that grow in rocky soil are those who "believe for a while, but in the time of testing they fall away" (Luke 8:13).

When children leave home for college or their own apartments, some of them fall away from their faith. They don't withstand the challenges to their childhood beliefs. Root your daughter's Christian faith in good soil by grounding her in a deep understanding of the gospel, the Ten Commandments, the catechisms, and Christian writings.

When your daughter is away from home, she will make wiser choices if she remembers how Jesus' love has been "poured out" in her heart and if you have taught her how the commandments apply to her life. The fifth commandment tells her how to treat her teachers—with respect. The eighth commandment tells her how to take an exam—not to cheat. The seventh commandment tells her what to do on a date—behave chastely. The fourth commandment tells her where she should go on Sunday—to worship God.

The catechisms and confessions provide a reliable framework for your daughter's faith. Catechisms are questions and answers that summarize what the Bible teaches. The confessions are mini-courses in theology. The more she knows what the church has believed down through the ages, the less she will be disturbed by every new idea, a coworker who thinks Christianity is stupid, a college professor who likes to rattle Christians, or a cult leader who calls out, "Follow me."

Missionary biographies can show your daughter what lives dedicated to God look like, challenge her to serve God, and help her put her own life and problems in perspective. Commentaries help her understand the Bible, and books on theology help her apply the Scriptures. Introduce your daughter to books that will inspire her imagination toward greater love for God.

Encourage Good Character

It is easy for girls today to get their priorities turned around. They improve their outside appearance with diets, new clothes, and make-up but neglect the inner beauty of good character.

Good character comes from God. The Holy Spirit causes the fruit of love, joy, peace, patience, kindness, goodness, faithfulness, gentleness, and self-control (Gal. 5:22–23) to grow. But you can help your daughter practice these fruits by what you encourage and discourage. When you remind her to control her temper, you encourage patience. When you teach her to share, you encourage love. When you help her keep her promises, you encourage faithfulness.

Mary takes her children with her to visit the elderly in nursing homes. The children prepare songs to entertain the residents and talk to bedridden patients. Mary is teaching her children to be kind, to love their neighbor (Lev. 19:18), to visit the sick (Matt. 25:34–40), and to honor their elders (Lev. 19:32). By your example, instruction, and discipline, you can help your daughter carry out her responsibilities to God and neighbor, and so help her to build good character.

Our responsibilities as parents can at times seem overwhelming. But sanctification is essentially the work of God, both in us and in our children (Phil. 1:6; 1 Thess. 5:23; Heb. 13:20–21). Jesus is the vine, we and our children are the branches, and the Father is the vinedresser (John 15:1–17). He shapes us as parents, and he shapes our children. God will enable you to be a tool for good when you seek him first. If he gives you the food and clothes you need (Matt. 6:25–34), how much more will he give you the abilities to train your daughter in the way she should go.

For Further Thought and Discussion

1. What habits lead to godliness? What are the benefits of memorizing Scripture? Of prayer? Of church attendance? Of helping others?
2. Read Matthew 5:17–48; Romans 13:8–10; and James 2:8–12. How should a Christian use the Ten Commandments? How could knowing the commandments help your daughter make the right decisions?

3. Read Romans 8:29; Galatians 5:22–25; and Colossians 3:1–4:6. How did Jesus show the fruit of the Spirit? How can we show the fruit of the Spirit? Do you see the fruit of the Spirit growing in yourself? In your daughter?

4. Read Galatians 5:16–26; Ephesians 4:17–6:9; and Colossians 3:1–4:6. What characterizes the old self? What characterizes the new self? Who produces the characteristics of the new self? What is the believer's responsibility?

5. Read John 15:1–17; Philippians 1:6; 2:13; 1 Thessalonians 5:23; and Hebrews 13:20–21. What promises do you find for you and for your daughter? What responsibilities? What items for prayer? How do these verses encourage you in your role as parent?

6. How are you instilling the habits of prayer, Bible reading, and church attendance in your daughter? How can you help her practice the fruit of the Spirit and good works?

PART 3

The Way of Wisdom

Points for Prayer

🎵 Pray that God would make you a wise parent.

🎵 Pray that your daughter would know what God wants her to know and do what God wants her to do.

"Folly is bound up in the heart of a child, but the rod of discipline will drive it far from him." —Proverbs 22:15

CHAPTER 6

Remember She Is Foolish

Have you ever wondered how any child lives to adulthood? From the day they become mobile, children seem to attract accidents and mishaps. They make foolish choices and get themselves into all sorts of scrapes, difficulties, and dilemmas. As they get older, they can get themselves into worse troubles than skinned knees or broken arms, and they can damage more than just their bodies. Wisdom does not come naturally to children; on the contrary, "foolishness is bound up in the heart of a child" (Prov. 22:15 NASB). This is self-evident to any grownup, but rarely to the child.

Children aren't the only ones who are foolish—outgrowing folly is a lifelong process for all of us. But youth and folly naturally go together, and folly seems to reach its acme in the teenage years when children also seem able to do the worst and most lasting damage to themselves. Would you rather your daughter crashed her bicycle at 6 miles per hour or a car at 60 miles per hour? Which can influence her more, a bad playmate on the block at age six or a bad boyfriend at sixteen?

To limit the damage your daughter can do to herself through her own folly, it is important to begin teaching her early to act wisely, to avoid recklessness, to choose wholesome friends, to gain knowledge and exercise prudence, to listen to advice and accept guidance, and to love the Lord and hate evil (see Prov. 1:1–7).

What Is Wisdom?

"What is wisdom?" I ask my Sunday school class. "Wisdom is knowing what God wants me to know and doing what God wants me to do," the children reply.[1] Wisdom is not merely what we know; it is also what we do. Wisdom is not the ability to explain philosophy or mathematics. Rather, it is insight, discernment, good judgment, and a wise course of action. Wisdom is shown by doing what God commands.

Wisdom is like a triangle, with one corner labeled spiritual, one intellectual, and one moral. Wisdom is spiritual because it begins with a right relationship with God, intellectual because wisdom is knowing the right things, and moral because wisdom is doing the right things. The spiritual, intellectual, and moral dimensions of wisdom are interrelated; without one, we do not really have the others.

The Bible describes two kinds of "wisdom": the false wisdom of men and the true wisdom that comes from God (1 Cor. 1:18–2:16; James 3:13–18). The most intelligent people can be fools, for the fool is the person who says in his heart, "There is no God" (Pss. 14:1; 53:1). The fool may know many true things, explain complicated theories, and even display practical common sense. Yet, if he denies God, he has become a fool—he thinks the wrong way, and he comes to the wrong conclusions (Rom. 1:18–32).

Because the fool does not fear God, he takes sin lightly (Ps. 36:1–4). He "thinks and acts as if he could safely disregard the eternal principles of God's righteousness."[2] He lives as he pleases, and, like the rich fool who stored up things on earth but not with God, he does not expect to face God's judgment (Luke 12:13–21).

Wisdom equips us to live by God's commands (Deut. 4:5–6). As we are confronted by the messages, temptations, problems, and conflicts of the world, wisdom answers the question, How are we to live in this world?[3]

The Book of Virtues

The book of Proverbs illustrates wisdom and its opposite, folly. Proverbs contains lessons and examples to make us and our children wise. The first nine chapters contain a father's advice to his son. "Listen, my son," Solomon begins. Listen to your father's instruction and your mother's teaching (1:8). My son, do not forget (3:1); pay attention (5:1); gain understanding (4:1); keep my words (7:1). Proverbs is the original Book of Virtues, stories and sayings that illustrate for our children the "essentials of good character," "what the virtues look like, what they are in practice, how to recognize them, and how they work."[4]

Solomon lists the essential characteristics of the wise man in 1:2–7, and then Proverbs demonstrates these qualities and their opposites throughout the book. The wise man is self-disciplined, but the fool is self-indulgent. The wise man has understanding and good judgment, but the fool makes bad choices. The wise man welcomes advice and rebuke, but the fool is arrogant and despises instruction. The wise man does good to others, but the fool is dangerous to those around him. The wise man prospers, but the fool is self-destructive. The wise man fears God and hates sin, but the fool says there is no God. Wisdom comes from God; foolishness comes naturally.

If Solomon's list of virtues describes our own children, how happy we will be—a wise child is a joy to her parents (23:24–25). "My son, if your heart is wise, then my heart will be glad; my inmost being will rejoice when your lips speak what is right" (23:15–16).

Though much in the world has changed since Solomon's day, people still have the same nature. And so our children face the same hazards as Solomon's son did: the wrong friends, sex outside marriage, substance abuse, pressure to go along with the crowd, violence and crime, envy and quarreling, laziness, and disregard for authority. Again and again, Proverbs tells parents to instruct and discipline their children. Why? Because children are naturally foolish.

Application *Read the book of Proverbs during family devotions. Point out the examples of good and bad character, wisdom and foolishness, and their consequences. Talk about how we see the same sorts of foolishness and wisdom today and why your daughter should want to be wise. Discuss how these wise sayings apply to her everyday situations.*

Your Daughter Is Foolish

Write Proverbs 22:15 on your hand or your shirt cuff—you'll need it: "Folly is bound up in the heart of a child." That will help you understand why she wants to date the boy who was banned from a youth group party when he showed up with marijuana. It will give you the conviction you need to say no when she wants to buy a dress that is too short or go to the movies with friends you don't really trust. It is an important factor when you are wondering, *Should I let her do that or not?*

The summer before Ellie entered seventh grade, I studied the book of Proverbs, and it was the best preparation I could have had. I don't think I would have been ready for the up and down emotions, the serious late-night talks, or the things she asked us if she could do, without the firm conviction that *children really are foolish.*

Some folly in a child is simple lack of knowledge and experience. An infant must learn about the world she has been born into: that a cat will scratch if she pulls his tail, that a stove is hot, and that if she jumps down the stairs, she will fall. She doesn't yet know about gravity, heat transference, or the dispositions of cats.

But the greater part of folly flows from the sin nature, from lack of faith in God, from lack of self-discipline, and from arrogant pride. Because, as Proverbs 1–9 shows, the young are inclined to folly, they are apt to be in the wrong places and to surround themselves with others as young, inexperienced, and foolish as themselves. And while they are still searching for truth, they believe they alone have the answers. They don't see the risks and dangers, and they have naïve expectations. They are self-absorbed. They do things they later regret.

Children show the folly in their hearts by their actions and decisions. Left to themselves—without instruction and discipline—children do some stupid, self-indulgent, destructive things. While our children often delight us with their sweetness and with hearts tender toward God, there is often an amazing correspondence between the characteristics of the fool described in Proverbs and the young.

No child is foolish all the time, and we do outgrow some foolishness as we mature. Family psychologist John Rosemond often asks parents of teens whether they themselves "did something fairly bad" as teenagers.[5] It's a good reminder that children today aren't really more foolish than we were at their age, though they may have opportunities to express it that we didn't have. But just as we *were* foolish, they now *are*, and they need guidance to grow into wise adults. If we understand how sinful folly has affected us, we'll be better prepared to counteract its effect on our daughters.

Application *Memorize Proverbs 22:15: "Folly is bound up in the heart of a child, but the rod of discipline will drive it far from him." Use it as a guiding principle in raising your daughter. Ask yourself: How does this problem show the foolishness in her heart? If I allow this, am I helping her to be wise or letting her continue foolishly? Can she come to harm from her own foolishness here? What do I need to do in this situation to help her grow wiser?*

Fools Are Downright Stupid

Children Lack Knowledge and Experience. Children say some of the funniest things out of ignorance. After a tour of duty in Germany, a family packed to return to the United States. Three-year-old Joan watched her family's belongings disappear into boxes "to go to America." To amuse Joan, her mother blew soap bubbles that popped and disappeared. But Joan knew where the bubbles had gone—"Bubbles go to America."

Lack of knowledge isn't always funny. Children do foolish, even harmful, things through inexperience. Children take unnecessary risks because they don't have enough experience to realize the dangers.

Teenagers don't have the experience to put either their problems or their successes in perspective. They go quickly from emotional highs to emotional lows and back again. To a teenager, almost any problem can seem catastrophic, permanent, and insurmountable. Young love can be especially traumatic. A teenage girl sees each new boyfriend as the love of her life, and each breakup as proof that life is over because she will *never* have another boyfriend, *ever*.

The teen who thinks she will never get another boyfriend may do anything to keep the one she has: hang out with a bad crowd because they are his friends, drink and smoke to fit in, have sex to please him, even put up with verbal or physical abuse.

Children Do Stupid Things. A friend called one night to say that her son had been in an accident. A group of teenage boys out on a Friday night had crowded into a truck with some of them riding in the truck bed, and the boys in the back decided to jump out at each traffic light. Jumping out before the truck stopped, the boy caught his foot, smashed into the pavement, and broke his jaw. The boy learned from his mistake, but some people make the same mistake over and over.

A friend's daughter seemed to attract bad boyfriends as if by magnetism. She had established a pattern: she broke up with one boyfriend and, before her parents could breathe a sigh of relief, brought home another just as bad or even worse. Not learning from her mistakes, she always thought she could change the next boy into a responsible young man. It never happened. The wise man gains understanding and knowledge (1:2, 4–5) through study, observation, and experience. The fool never learns from his own experiences, much less from the mistakes of others.

The wise man has insight and discernment to see accurately what is not evident to the average person, but the fool does not see what is right before him and evident to anyone paying attention. "Wisdom calls aloud in the street," but fools and mockers ignore her (1:20–33; 8:1–9:12). Wild birds have sense enough to see a net spread in full view, but not so the fool (1:17). Children don't see the obvious dangers. Young teens smoke in spite of warning labels on the packages and use drugs in spite of Just Say No clubs at school. The fool lacks judgment (10:21).

Children Are Naïve. The fool is naïve; he believes anything and is easily deceived (14:15). It's easy to get young children to believe all sorts of wild imaginings, such as animals that talk and toys that come to life. Though the innocence of childhood can be a fun thing, we want our children to grow in wisdom and make informed judgments. A naïve teenager will believe the boyfriend who says, "I love you; have sex with me now." A wise teenager will know that love must be expressed according to God's commands, and she will be less likely to fall for a line.

Children Are Reckless. The fool keeps going right into danger (22:3). Fools view warning signs as an invitation to find out what's back there. The fool thinks: "That ice will hold." "I don't need to slow down for that curve." "How dangerous can swimming in a quarry be?" "The tide doesn't look that bad."

Teenagers are notoriously reckless. They try alcohol, cigarettes, and illegal drugs just to see what they taste like or what effect they will have. They have more automobile accidents than any other age group. Trying to impress their friends, they will try almost anything on a dare.

Children Have Poor Judgment. The fool chooses foolish and dangerous companions (1:10ff.; 2:12). Many parents are baffled when their children use drugs or suddenly get bad grades at school, when their daughters get pregnant or take up smoking. Often these parents have ignored the friends their children hang out with.

The wise man exercises prudence, discretion, and good judgment (1:2–5). The fool is imprudent in practical matters (6:1ff.; 6:32ff.) and has bad judgment (6:32; 7:7). The fool doesn't handle money wisely (17:16, 18). Give your daughter ten dollars to use any way she wants. The younger she is, the more candy she will buy. Children don't even choose nutritious food if left to themselves; they would much rather eat cookies than green beans.

The wise man gives thought to his own steps (14:15), but the fool gives no thought to his way of life (5:6). Children rarely consider the consequences of what they do. The fool makes hasty decisions (19:2), and so do children. Just like the fool, children often answer before listening (18:13).

Fools Are Self-Indulgent

Children Are Impatient. Children expect instant results and instant gratification. Time seems longer to a child than to an adult, especially on trips and before Christmas or her birthday. A year from now is a lifetime. One Christmas, we bought sleds for our girls, and they were anxious to try them out. But there was one problem: it hadn't snowed yet. Within a week, Sarah was declaring, "It will never snow again!"

Children Don't Consider the Future. Just as in Aesop's fable of the ants and the grasshopper, the fool lives for the moment, but the wise man thinks about the future. Like Esau, children can be willing to trade a better future for the pleasures of the present. The fool uses up all he has without saving for later (Prov. 21:20).

Children Lack Self-Control. The fool despises discipline (1:7) and does whatever feels good. If drugs or alcohol or cigarettes make you feel better, the fool says, use them. The fool does not exercise self-control. He becomes a drunkard (20:1), a glutton (23:19–21), or a sluggard (24:30–34). He indulges his sexual desires outside marriage (7:1ff.; 29:3). But the wise man is self-disciplined (1:3) and patient (14:29; 19:11).

The wise man keeps his anger under control (17:27; 29:11), but the fool is quick-tempered (14:17, 29) and gives full vent to his anger (29:11). He shows his annoyance at once (12:16). Children are quick to anger, and they act out their frustrations.

Children Lack Discretion. The fool speaks and acts rashly and recklessly (13:3; 14:16). He does or says whatever comes into his head without thinking about the consequences. Art Linkletter interviewed young children in a segment of his television show, called "Kids Say the Darnedest Things"—and they did. Sometimes what they said was amazingly (and amusingly) perceptive. But often what came out of their mouths was striking for its youthful indiscretion. As the fool "gushes folly" (15:2), so did many a youngster on that program.

Fools Think They Know It All

Children Think They Know Everything. "When I was a boy of fourteen, my father was so ignorant I could hardly stand to have the old man around," said Mark Twain. "But when I got to be twenty-one, I was astonished at how much he had learned in seven years." In like fashion, I was amazed at how wise my own parents seemed once I had children of my own.

About the same time children try to be seen with their parents as little as possible, they also tend to think their parents know nothing—at least of any value to them. They listen to their peers more than to their parents.

Convinced that they know it all, the young by and large discount the wisdom and experience of older generations. Because an idea is new to them, the young assume that no one else has thought of it or understands it better than they. The fool is arrogant (21:24), and "the mocker disdains everyone else."[6] The fool is too proud to accept advice (13:10). With a roll of their eyes and a loud sigh, often teenagers show what they think about advice.

"No, do it myself!" is a developmental stage that frustrates parents of two year olds, because children that young aren't able to do most things without help. By the time they are teenagers, they are really hungry for independence, but they never outgrow the need for advice and guidance. Your sophisticated teenager still needs your guidance. Only the fool thinks independence means never having to take advice. His own way seems right to the fool (12:15).

"A fool finds no pleasure in understanding but delights in airing his own opinions" (18:2) is a good description of many teenagers. They are generous with their opinions, but often those opinions are not well thought out or even based on reality.

Children Would Rather Play. The wise man is always learning, but the fool hates knowledge (1:29). By April, most children hate school and would rather play than attend classes, study, and do homework. Think back to your days as a student. I liked the easy teachers who let me goof off and do what I wanted. And I grumbled about the teachers who gave a lot of homework and hard tests. But years later I appreciate most the hard teachers who demanded my best. Ignorance may be bliss, but it is also an invitation to foolishness.

Fools Are Self-Destructive

Children Think They Are Immortal. A teenager skied off a precipice and into a snowdrift, where he wasn't found until too late. His friends had tried to discourage him from the dangerous stunt, but he had done it before, and he was convinced he could do it again. He never expected to die.

A sixteen year old behind the wheel of a car thinks he can never die. The thirteen year old who smokes thinks she will never get lung cancer, or if she does, the doctor will just cure her. A boy out hiking a steep and slippery trail never dreams he might fall. Sexually active teens don't expect pregnancies, and teens who drink alcohol on prom night never envision having a car accident. Children do not anticipate bad consequences.

Dark tans are back in among college students, *The Wall Street Journal* reported. Young people know the dangers, but don't care. "Wrinkles? That's years away. Melanoma? The odds are low." "It's like drinking," explains Jen; "you know it's bad for you but you do it anyway." "You are going to die of something eventually," says Nichole; "you might as well die tanned."[7]

Children haven't considered their own mortality. A child can't imagine growing old; she hasn't learned to number her days (Ps. 90:12).

Children Hurt Themselves. The wise woman "builds her house," but the fool tears it down with her own hands (Prov. 14:1). The fool comes to poverty (13:18) and ruin (19:3) caused by his own actions (1:18–19). Likewise, teenagers who drink and drive risk accidents; the young woman who buys a car she can't afford falls into poverty; teenagers who engage in sexual sin bring about pregnancies and sexually transmitted diseases; children who defy their teachers earn detentions and trips to the principal. The fool brings about his own punishment (14:3; 18:6; 19:3).

The fool is a danger to himself and others (13:20; 17:12). He is not content to get himself in trouble—he wants company. Children will get into mischief together that each would never dream of doing by herself. Easily persuaded to go along with the crowd, they will do something they know to be wrong because "everyone else" does it.

The fool hates himself (15:32), but the wise man loves himself ("his own soul," 19:8). Between the ages of eleven and thirteen, girls in our culture tend to hate their bodies and often themselves. They become discontent with how they are made, and they make bad choices. Their grades drop, they become discipline problems, they have unsavory friends, they become pregnant, they use drugs. The fool hates himself or his own soul because he doesn't know God or consider how to please God.

Application *Teach your daughter that when she doesn't obey God, she is really hurting herself and that when she obeys God, she is doing good to herself. Teach her that those who know God are happy. Have her memorize Psalm 144:15b: "Blessed are the people whose God is the LORD" and Proverbs 19:8a: "He who gets wisdom loves his own soul."*

Children Do Things They Regret. The wise man will inherit honor (Prov. 3:35; 13:18), but the fool inherits shame (13:18) and a life filled with regrets (5:11–14). Many from the sixties generation are now regretting their experimentation with marijuana, either because they have a hard time explaining it to their own children or because the media are making it front-page news. The phrase "youthful indiscretions" probably makes us all cringe, because we have done things we hope no one ever finds out about.

Fools Say There Is No God

Children Are Selfish. Any child thinks the universe revolves around her. Children are selfish and self-absorbed.

Abe grew up in a large family, and even now he is meticulous about cutting pies into the exact number of pieces as the people in the room. In his family his mother didn't allow leftovers, because it caused too many arguments over who got an extra piece. For children, nothing can really be equal enough.

Jealousy and sibling rivalry are symptoms that nearly every child wants to be an only child. Siblings resent the attention a brother or sister gets. Just as cakes are never divided equally enough, neither is a parent's attention. Erma Bombeck wrote about trying to give her children Christmas gifts of equal value lest her other children find out that she spent more on one. Each time she tried to even up the values, one child came out ahead, which meant she had to go shopping again, and again, and again—it was a never-ending task.

A child thinks only about her own feelings. She can wound the feelings of everyone around her without one ounce of empathy, but her own feelings are fragile. She expects better treatment than she gives.

Children Look for Approval from Their Peers. A group of seventh graders were huddled and whispering in the hall. "I don't want this," one of them said as she took the small bag. A teacher wandered over and asked, "Don't want what?" Before the end of the day, sixteen seventh graders had been caught with marijuana. One child had brought it to school and handed it around to her friends.

Why did the girl who said "I don't want this" take the bag anyway? What makes a child go along with the crowd, give in to peer pressure, or show off to impress others? She is looking for approval in the wrong place. She is trying to please her friends rather than God.

The fool does not fear God or appreciate the power of God's anger (Ps. 90:11). When a child goes along with the crowd, even in doing something she knows to be wrong, she fears her peers more than she fears God.

Fools break God's commands: they commit sexual sins (7:1ff.; 29:3), are quick to anger (12:16; 14:17, 29; 29:11), follow their own way (12:15; 28:26), are proud and arrogant (11:2; 21:24), spread slander (10:18), delight in doing wrong (2:14), and rush into sin (1:16). "The schemes of folly are sin" (24:9). Folly is sin because it is acting contrary to the all-wise God.

The Consequences of Folly

Sin carries consequences. It has natural results that no one can escape, even by repentance and forgiveness. If a teen becomes pregnant, she can repent of the sexual sin and receive forgiveness, but she will still be pregnant. The pregnancy is a natural consequence of the sexual sin. A drunkard may repent and never drink again, but if he has damaged his liver, he will still have health problems. A repentant gambler will still have lost his money.

In addition, God also punishes sin by "divine enactment."[8] That is, some of the misery of sin comes directly from God, in unhappiness, guilt, and mental anguish; natural calamities; spiritual separation from God; and, finally, hell itself. If the pregnant teen doesn't repent, she will suffer from a guilty conscience. She may be depressed, experience conflict with her family, fight with her boyfriend, and have trouble in school. She will continue to make bad choices, because she does not have the wisdom of God to guide her. Without repentance she will only see her situation get worse, because God will continue to punish her sin.

Sin is self-destructive. Wisdom says, "Whoever fails to find me harms himself; all who hate me love death" (Prov. 8:36). Because the fool disregards God and his law, he brings ruin to himself (1:32; 6:32; 10:21; 15:32), danger to his companions (1:10–19; 13:20), and grief to his parents (10:1; 17:21, 25; 19:13; 29:15).

Tragically, the consequences of folly are spread over the front pages of our newspapers. "An Allentown youth was shot and killed in an attempted armed robbery at a convenience store in the city yesterday—one day shy of his 16th birthday," began a front-page story.[9] The other two robbers, who escaped injury, were in their twenties. The teenager thought "hanging out with an older crowd . . . was cool."[10] This boy, like the fool in Proverbs 1:10–19, joined with violent companions, and his end, just as in verses 18 and 19, was his own death.

Less sensational stories fill the back pages of the newspaper. A teenager drives drunk and kills his friend. Children playing with matches start a house fire. Children wade too far out into the river and are drowned. A high school student makes napalm from instructions he found on the Internet and takes it to school. High school basketball players caught drinking are suspended from the team. Other incidents of folly never make the newspapers, although they are reflected in the statistics on teen pregnancy, smoking, or drug use. Through poor judgment, children put themselves in danger, and often they bring grief to themselves, their companions, and their parents.

Children need wisdom. If we look back at the characteristics of the fool, we all can think of examples of adults who fit these categories as much as children do. And we don't want our children to become foolish adults as well.

For Further Thought and Discussion

1. Read Proverbs 1:1–7. What are the characteristics of those who are wise? What are the characteristics of fools? Give some examples of each. Which characteristics of wisdom are your daughter's strengths? Which are her weaknesses?

2. Read Psalm 14:1–4; and Proverbs 3:7; 8:13; 9:10. Why does true wisdom have a spiritual, an intellectual, and a moral element? How does the fool show that he does not fear God?

3. Read Proverbs 8:36; 14:1; and 22:3. In what ways are fools self-destructive? In what ways is folly dangerous? Why is it foolish to take sin lightly?

4. Read Proverbs 5:21–23; 9:7–9; 10:18–21, 23; and 24:9. How are fools and the wicked alike? Why?

5. Read Proverbs 22:15. Why is it important for parents to understand folly? What foolishness do you see in your daughter's heart? How can you discourage foolish behavior in your daughter and encourage her to grow wise?

6. Why is the book of Proverbs still so applicable in today's modern world?

Points for Prayer

🎵 Pray that your daughter would love God with all her heart, body, mind, and soul and hate sin.

🎵 Pray that God would strengthen your daughter to resist temptation.

"To fear the LORD is to hate evil; I hate pride and arrogance, evil behavior and perverse speech." —Proverbs 8:13

CHAPTER 7

Teach Her to Love God and Hate Sin

Many a little girl wants to be National Velvet. The movie makes it look easy, as if she can just hop on a horse and win a steeplechase. In fact, it is downright dangerous for the inexperienced. That kind of riding comes only through years of training and practice.

Wisdom, like the ability to jump fences, is not acquired without training and practice. If God placed wisdom full and complete into our children's heads and hearts in an instant, parents would save many sleepless nights. But he doesn't.

Wisdom must be learned over time, but it does have a beginning: "The fear of the LORD is the beginning of wisdom, and knowledge of the Holy One is understanding" (Prov. 9:10; see also 1:7; Ps. 111:10). The first and indispensable step in gaining wisdom is knowing the Lord.

How can your daughter know God? Through his Son, Jesus Christ. When the Philippian jailer asked, "What must I do to be saved?" Paul and Silas replied, "Believe in the Lord Jesus" (Acts 16:30–31). Believing in the Lord Jesus means continually trusting that his death on the cross has fully paid for all your sins. "For all have sinned and fall short of the glory of God. . . .

[And] the wages of sin is death, but the gift of God is eternal life in Christ Jesus our Lord" (Rom. 3:23; 6:23).

Don't assume that your daughter has come to saving faith in Jesus Christ because she goes to church or Sunday school. She may know a lot *about* Jesus and yet not understand what it means to know *him*. Look for opportunities to discuss and clarify the gospel, and encourage her to trust in Jesus.

If your daughter professes faith in Christ, look for signs that she is growing in her faith. Is her heart tender to the things of God? Is she learning to respond with repentance when you show her where she is not following Jesus' example? Does she accept guidance from the Scriptures? Is she asking God for help with her problems at school? Is she reading the Bible and asking questions that show her interest in understanding more about God?

Make it your goal to raise a daughter who will be characterized by wisdom: by self-discipline, understanding, knowledge, insight, discernment, prudence, discretion, and good judgment; by adding to her learning and receiving advice; by doing what is right and dealing fairly with others; by fearing the Lord and seeking the Lord's guidance (Prov. 1:2–7). Wisdom of this kind grows as she learns to love God. Remember that wisdom is a "triangle" with three inseparable corners—one labeled spiritual (a right relationship with God), one intellectual (knowing the right things), and one moral (doing the right things). To teach your daughter to be wise, you must teach her to fear God, to know the Scriptures, to obey God's commands, and to hate sin.

Teach Her to Fear God

Wisdom begins with knowledge *and fear* of the Lord. Those who truly know God fear him. That is, they respect his authority, power, and holiness; they remember that he hates and punishes sin; and they are always aware that Jesus paid for their sins by suffering on the cross.

Those who fear God want to please him and to avoid sin. "To fear the LORD is to hate evil" (Prov. 8:13a; see also 14:16). A daughter who fears the Lord will act more wisely, because she knows that God, unlike her parents, is everywhere and sees everything she does. Nothing can be hidden from God (Heb. 4:13).

How can you teach your daughter to fear the Lord without making her afraid of him? Focus on Jesus. God's love demonstrated in Jesus (Rom. 5:8) will keep her from fear that God will punish her as her sins deserve (Rom. 8:1; 1 John 4:18). And yet it will remind her that God is holy. The more she understands God's love in Jesus, the more she will revere him.

Teach Her the Scriptures

To know God intimately, your daughter must also know the Scriptures. God has revealed himself through his Word, and through his Word he reveals his will and gives wisdom. "The unfolding of your words gives . . . understanding to the simple" (Ps. 119:130), that is, to those who lack understanding and judgment (Prov. 9:4–6). Wisdom doesn't come in a mystical *poof!* It comes through understanding the Scriptures (Ps. 119:97–104).

Encourage your daughter to know the Scriptures through Bible reading, study, and memorization. Remember that God's Word is living and active (Heb. 4:12).

Teach Her to Do What the Scriptures Say

"We know that we have come to know him if we obey his commands. The man who says, 'I know him,' but does not do what he commands is a liar, and the truth is not in him" (1 John 2:3–4; see also John 14:21, 23). Your daughter's intimacy with God is revealed by what she does (James 2:14–26), and so is her wisdom (3:13–18).

In the parable of the builders, the foolish builder heard Jesus' words but did not put them into practice (Luke 6:46–49). The wise man is the one who puts Jesus' words into practice: A wise man tells the truth. A wise child obeys her parents. A wise wife avoids adultery. A wise teen doesn't use drugs.

We all *know* more than we *do,* however, because it is easier to know than to do. The easy part of the softball coach's job is telling youngsters how to stand at the plate and hold a bat or how to hold the glove in the outfield. The hard part is getting pint-sized players to hit the ball or make the catch. The doing comes through the coach's continued instruction and training and through the child's practice, discipline, and hard work.

We already know we should not lie, steal, commit sexual sin, or hate our brothers, and it's easy enough to read the Bible, learn the Ten Commandments, or memorize Scripture verses. The hard part is not lying when the truth is embarrassing, not stealing when the money is lying on the table, not giving in to the passions of the moment, and not getting angry with the brother who doesn't seem fair. Just as a ball player needs to practice catching pop flies, your daughter needs to practice doing what God wants her to do until it becomes a habit.

You are not just teaching her a new skill, however. It's much easier teaching her to catch a fly ball than to tell the truth when it hurts. As you teach her God's commandments (Deut. 6:7–9), pray that the Holy Spirit would work in her so that she would obey them.

Teach Her to Hate Sin

The more we love God, the more we will hate sin. We will become increasingly like our Lord, thinking and acting the way he did (Rom. 12:2; Col. 3:1–17). We will be transformed from hating God's law to loving God's law, from loving sin to hating sin. Your daughter is constantly confronted with the choice between loving God and loving sin. She cannot have it both ways.

That doesn't mean believers can't sin. We do and will as long as we are in this world. And so will our daughters. But a true believer hates her sin and wants to outgrow sinful habits. One way to teach your daughter to hate sin is by showing her what sin and its consequences look like. The "advantage" of living in a sinful world is that there are examples of sin all around us. Solomon used these as teaching examples. You can too.

What Does Sin Look Like?

Chuck was a professor at a university that had a reputation as a "party school." When his children were teenagers, he took them to parties on campus to show them how students made fools of themselves. Chuck's kids witnessed drunks throwing up in the bushes or on their dates' shoes. They saw girls being propositioned. They saw people engaged in frantic activity but not having fun. "See; this is what sin looks like," Chuck said. His children saw that sin is not glamorous or even really fun.

While under the power of sin, people think they are having more fun than they really are. John and I went to a trade show held in Las Vegas. One night we entered a casino just to look around on our way to a concert. As we were walking through, John said to me, "Let's see if we can find ten people who look as if they're having fun." We even counted employees, but we couldn't find ten people who were smiling, much less really enjoying themselves. Yet if you had asked them, most of the gamblers would have said that they came to have fun. After they got home, they may even have said they did have fun. But their faces told a different story. They showed that sin does not make us happy.

One weekend at college, just before I became a Christian, I observed two groups of people: a fraternity party and a Christian student organization. Unlike the people at the fraternity party, the Christians were having real fun—and they had nothing to regret the next morning. The contrast made a powerful impression on me. I knew which group I wanted to be like, and it wasn't the party crowd. Viewing the ugliness of sin as an "outside observer" can make a powerful and lasting impression on your children too.

You don't have to take your children to fraternity parties or casinos to show them sin and its consequences. Just look around your neighborhood or listen to your daughter describe her schoolmates. Point out the consequences of sin and help her think through the results. "Poor Sharon! She's made life very difficult for herself by having sex before marriage. Now she has a baby. It's going to be hard for her to finish high school. She may have a hard time finding a job. How is she going to take care of this baby? What does she need to do now?" "Harry is always fighting with the other children. Do they like Harry very much? How should Harry treat his friends?"

Sin is never a good choice. Your daughter can learn to hate what sin does to the sinner. Seeing the consequences of sin helps her understand how much it violates God's good design for his creation.

One danger in using other people's sins to show your daughter how not to live is that she could become like the Pharisee who prayed, "God, I thank you that I am not like other men" (see Luke 18:9–14). Sarah sometimes takes a "what's wrong with them!" attitude. Don't let your daughter forget that the temptation that overtakes others would also overcome her if God's grace did not prevent it (1 Cor. 10:13). Show her sin in others not to make her arrogant and judgmental but to make her aware of the results of sin, to make her humble and on guard, to point out *her* need to rely on Jesus for forgiveness and on the Holy Spirit for power over sin.

Another danger in showing your daughter what sin looks like is that she might actually be attracted to or get caught up in it. Be careful what you expose her to and in what context. Though a picture may be worth a thousand words, pornographic movies are not a good choice for showing her what sexual sin looks like. She doesn't need to experiment with drugs to find out that they are harmful, visit a crack house, or join a street gang. She doesn't need to know everything there is to know about sin in all its forms of depravity.

She does need to know that human nature inclines toward sin and that Jesus gives us power over sin. Sin is enticing, but through the Holy Spirit, we can resist sin and do what is right. Sin is in our nature. At times we will *want* to sin, but we do not *have* to sin.

Often we sin because we don't have a plan *not* to, and so the heat of the moment overtakes us. Most teenagers don't plan to have sex on any particular date, but one thing leads to another. Part of teaching your daughter to hate sin is giving her a plan for resisting the power of sin. Avoiding bad habits, bad situations, and bad companions (see chapter 8) will help her avoid opportunities for sin, but temptation will still present itself at parties, on dates, at school, in everyday life. Prepare your daughter ahead of time to resist sin.

"Which Way Is the Exit?"

God never puts us in a place where we have to sin; he always provides "a way out" (1 Cor. 10:13), a way of escape from temptation. Where is the exit from temptation?

In Prayer. Since the Holy Spirit alone renews her heart, mind, and will to hate sin and want to do good, an indispensable part of your daughter's plan to avoid sin is prayer, both for God to keep temptation away from her and to give her power over temptation. But Christians often say, "I prayed, and nothing happened."

Explain to your daughter that when she prays, she must expect God to give her power over temptation—and then take action based on that faith (see James 1:5–8; 2:14–26). She feels pressured by her friends to wear short tops and low-fitting jeans, smoke cigarettes, and take drugs. She needs to pray—and find new friends. When she sees money she could steal, she should pray—and then turn and walk away. When she prays, God will give her the strength to do what is right.

In a Long-Term Perspective. Sin results from self-indulgence, doing what feels good without thinking about the consequences. Along with the spiritual fruit of self-control (Gal. 5:22–23), your daughter needs a long-term perspective, one that looks beyond temporary gratification. Sin is a "passing pleasure" (Heb. 11:25 NASB); sooner or later the guilt and consequences of sin wipe out any pleasure from it.

Encourage your daughter to consider, *How will I feel tomorrow? Will I regret doing this? Is this a passing pleasure that leads to guilt? If I do this, can my conscience be clear before the holy Lord? Do I want Jesus to see me doing this?* Teach her that nothing can be hidden from God (Heb. 4:13). No matter where she goes or how secret she thinks she is, God is there and knows what she is doing (Ps. 139:1–12; Prov. 5:21).

Application *Teach your daughter to stop and think,* Will I feel ashamed if I do this? Will it dampen my love for God? *Have her memorize Hebrews 4:13: "Nothing in all creation is hidden from God's sight. Everything is uncovered and laid bare before the eyes of him to whom we must give account."*

In a Good Offense. The full armor of God in Ephesians 6:10–18 provides one offensive weapon—the sword of the Spirit, the Word of God (v. 17). The more Scripture she has hidden in her heart, the better her defense. At the right time, the Holy Spirit will bring to mind the verse she needs for encouragement and strength to resist or for conviction of conscience to stop. When others in her group of friends are gossiping about a classmate, the Holy Spirit will remind her that the Lord hates a lying tongue, a false witness, and one who stirs up dissension (Prov. 6:16–19).

Scripture provides not only a weapon in her own heart but a defense against outside pressure. The one who says, "We shouldn't do this, because God says we shouldn't," will find that the group leaves her behind. Sinners don't want someone around who will give them guilty consciences.

Taking a stand will also lead to opportunities to tell others about Christ. Part of the armor of God is "feet fitted with the readiness that comes from the gospel of peace" (Eph. 6:15). Saying "I won't do this, because God says sex is for marriage only" can change the situation from fighting off hands to explaining the gospel—and the temptation to sin is taken away when the atmosphere changes.

In Mad Money. There was a time when a girl on a date carried a dime in her shoe so that she could call home if the date was awful or the boy was too fresh. This was "mad money"—if she got mad at her date, she had money to get herself home. This illustrates the last resort against temptation: If all else fails, if temptation becomes too strong to handle, get out of there! Run from the situation just as Joseph fled Potiphar's wife (Gen. 39:11–12).

When your daughter goes out, make sure she has "mad money." Make her a promise: "No matter where you are, I will always come and get you." Let her know she has options; she can always just leave the situation, and you will support her.

It takes courage to back away from a situation when not going along means losing face before her peers. Whether it's a party with alcohol and drugs or a first cigarette or sexual experimentation, she will face jeers and taunts if she doesn't go along. But Jesus said we should hate sin so much that we would pluck out an eye or cut off a hand rather than sin (Matt. 5:29–30). If she loves God, she will hate sin and love God's law, and she will show it by her actions. If she loves God and hates sin, she can endure a little peer harassment.

Use Conversation

"My son, listen; pay attention; do not forget; store up my commands; accept what I say; keep my words; give me your heart." In the first nine chapters of Proverbs, Solomon constantly calls his son to listen. Your daughter needs constant teaching and constant reminders to love God, hate sin, and do what she knows is right.

Proverbs 1–9 is not a conversation between father and son. It's more like a letter, and we can only imagine the son's responses. Most of our teaching, however, takes place face to face. In fact, eye contact is one of the most important elements of communication. Another is listening. Our daughters listen to us, but we also listen to them in order to find out what they are experiencing, thinking, and feeling. Unless you talk to your daughter regularly, you may not know that her classmates are already using drugs or having sexual experiences and that you need to reinforce her stand on these issues.

By talking with your daughter, you learn what is important to her. If she is concerned about not having dates on the weekend, use that as an opportunity to talk about patience and trusting God to bring the right person along at the right time. Talk about what kind of young man she wants to date and why. From what you learn, you can pray more specifically.

When you talk with your daughter, you find out which lessons have "taken" and which haven't yet. One of my Sunday school lessons was on the man who found a treasure in a field and sold everything he had to buy the field. One of my students was worried about a friend who was selfish and mean to others, and so we took a few minutes to talk about this. Then Heather decided to go home and tell her friend about her "greatest treasure," knowing Jesus. By giving her time to talk, I found out that the lesson had gone to her heart. She knew precisely what Jesus meant when he said, "The kingdom of heaven is like treasure . . ." (Matt. 13:44).

Use Real Life

Solomon observed the world around him, both people and animals, and used them to teach his son how to love God and avoid sin. Foolish youths do follow prostitutes (Prov. 7:6–27),

Solomon noticed. People have put up security for their neighbors (6:1–5). Jealous husbands have taken revenge (6:30–35). Robbers do get caught in their own traps (1:10–19). A lazy man can make up fantastic excuses to get out of work (22:13). People aren't always what they seem (13:7). Beauty isn't everything (11:22). Businessmen, gossips, ne'er do wells, the poor, the rich, good and bad wives, wise and foolish children, kings and servants—Solomon used them all.

Use the examples around you as well. People still lie, still spend their money foolishly, still commit sexual sins, still hoard their possessions. People still work hard, are kind to the needy, refuse bribes, and trust in the Lord, just as they did in Solomon's day. One teen thinks she can cheat a drug dealer and ends up dead. Another teen with a physical handicap works hard enough to make the high school swim team.

Solomon's examples are easy to remember. Who can forget the industrious ant, the pig with a gold nose ring, or the wife who is like dripping water? Faithfulness in marriage is like drinking from your own well (5:15); adultery, like scooping fire into your own lap (6:27); the fool who follows the prostitute, like an ox going to slaughter (7:22). How do children remember to be industrious? By remembering the ant. How does a girl remember that good character is better than beauty? By remembering the pig with a gold nose ring. Equip your daughter with the vivid examples of Proverbs.

Use the Ten Commandments

The Ten Commandments underlie the examples of wise and foolish behavior in Proverbs. The foolish youth who follows the prostitute breaks the seventh commandment. The robbers in chapter 1 break the sixth and eight commandments by murdering and stealing. The prudent man who overlooks an insult (12:16) keeps the sixth commandment by not hating his brother (Matt. 5:21–22). The generous man (Prov.

11:25–28) keeps the eighth commandment by giving to others (Eph. 4:28). The wise speaker (Prov. 12:17–19) keeps the ninth commandment. The man whose own way seems right to him (12:15) breaks the first and second commandments, but the man who leans on God (3:5–7) keeps them.

Teach your daughter to evaluate her actions by principles encapsulated in the Ten Commandments: *Is this keeping or breaking the commandments? Am I doing what the commandments require and avoiding what the commandments forbid? Which commandments bear on this action or decision? How can I obey those commandments in this situation?* The seventh commandment applies to how she dresses. The ninth commandment applies to how she talks about others. The first commandment applies to her relationships to her peers. The fool breaks God's commands, but the wise man applies them to everyday situations out of love for God.

Application *Ask your daughter to read through the book of Proverbs and look for how the verses apply the Ten Commandments. Make it a contest; for example, if she finds more than fifty examples of the Ten Commandments, you will take her out for ice cream or to the movies. Talk about the examples she finds and how those examples apply to her.*

Make Course Corrections

In the movie *Apollo 13*, the astronauts don't realize they are drifting off course. But ground control has a perspective the astronauts do not: the space craft will hit Earth's atmosphere at the wrong angle and either break up or skip off into space with no way to turn around. The astronauts have to make a course change.

Parents likewise have a perspective children do not. And when you see your daughter off course, you must correct her to keep her heading in the right direction, toward love for God and hatred of sin.

Your daughter's life can be like a ray in mathematics. A ray starts from a certain point and continues in the same direction into infinity. Two rays can start from the same point; but the longer we draw the lines, the farther apart the lines become. What seems like a small decision can, over time, make a huge difference in your daughter's life.

Robert Frost wrote a poem about two roads that diverged into a wood. As far as he could see down each road, the two looked about the same. But he chose the one less traveled, and because "way leads on to way," he never came back to that fork. As he looked back over his life, he saw that that choice "made all the difference."[1]

There are two roads in Scripture as well—the broad and the narrow: "Wide is the gate and broad is the road that leads to destruction, and many enter through it. But small is the gate and narrow the road that leads to life, and only a few find it" (Matt. 7:13–14). The small gate and narrow road are Jesus and his way (see Luke 13:22–30; John 14:6).

Growing up is a scary time for a girl. Everything is changing around her—her friends, her body, her activities and interests, what others expect of her. Her future is unclear. It is like standing in a murky stream and trying to walk forward without being able to see the bottom. All around her the water flows, moving, taking away the familiar and bringing change. The stream bed is uneven; there are loose rocks and holes. But under the water lies a path of solid rock, on which she can safely walk. Jesus is the Way and the Rock (Pss. 18:30–36; 62:1–2). Teach your daughter to love him and his way.

Application *Get a copy of Robert Frost's "The Road Not Taken" and read it with your daughter. Talk about what the poem means and how choices make a difference in our lives. Ask, How does way lead on to way? Why did he never come back to that same fork in the road? Compare the meaning of the poem to what Jesus says in Matthew 7:13–14. Talk about what kinds of choices are good and what kinds are bad. Have her memorize this poem.*

For Further Thought and Discussion

1. Read Proverbs 9:10. What is the fear of the Lord? Why is the fear of the Lord the beginning of wisdom? How does fear of the Lord lead us to obey him?

2. Read 1 John 4:16–18. Are love for and fear of God contradictory? What kind of fear of God should a Christian have? Not have?

3. Read Psalm 7:11 and Romans 1:18–32. Why does God hate sin?

4. Read 1 Corinthians 10:13. Then read Matthew 4:1–11; 6:9–13; 26:41; Ephesians 6:10–18; and Hebrews 4:13; 11:25. How can we resist sin?

5. Read Proverbs 1–9. If you were writing your daughter a letter of advice, what would you include? How would your letter be like Solomon's? How would it be different? What examples would you use?

6. Why do parents who ignore small behavioral problems see their children develop big ones? How can parents decide what behavior to encourage and what to discourage?

Point for Prayer

꒰ Pray that your daughter would love God's Word and grow in wisdom, discernment, maturity, and the fruit of the Spirit.

"Blessed is the man who does not walk in the counsel of the wicked or stand in the way of sinners or sit in the seat of mockers. But his delight is in the law of the Lᴏʀᴅ, and on his law he meditates day and night." —Psalm 1:1–2

CHAPTER 8

Teach Her to Make Wise Choices

Down the road from where I grew up stood an old farmhouse. It once belonged to my grandmother's sister, but no one had lived there as long as I could remember. Then along came kudzu. Within a few summers, house, trees, and yard were buried under waves of kudzu vines, and tendrils were threatening to cross the road into our fields.

Given a chance in the right climate, the kudzu vine grows sixty to one hundred feet a year. It takes over fields, swallows trees, and wraps up abandoned houses. Kudzu thrives under neglect, and once entrenched, it takes years to kill. It can be controlled only by regular maintenance such as mowing and pruning.[1]

Leaving your daughter to her own judgment is like not cutting back kudzu. Her situation could fast get out of control. Her well-being could be smothered by her own foolish choices as her life is taken over by folly the way Aunt Josie's house was taken over by kudzu.

Left to themselves, children make bad choices. Scripture says that our children lack good judgment (Prov. 22:15). Foolishness entangles their thinking, feeling, and acting. Parents, like a good gardener, need to be pruning the foolishness out so that it won't take over.

Teach Her to Avoid Bad Companions

Discrimination is a good thing. Not the sort that leads to judging people by the color of their skin, but the sort that leads to keeping away from bad companions.

Bad Friends

As mentioned earlier, one of the biggest mistakes parents make is letting their children hang out with the wrong friends. Get to know your daughter's friends. Do they treat adults with respect or contempt? Have you ever caught them in serious lies or deceptions? What do they talk about? Are they interested in activities you would rather your daughter didn't do, at least not at her age? Do they have any bad habits you don't want your daughter to take up? How does your daughter act when she is with them? If she is doing things you wouldn't allow, that is a sign she may have the wrong friends.

Bad companions "wear off" on the one who associates with them (1 Cor. 15:33). She adopts their language, dress, and attitudes. If they are disrespectful to their parents, she will become disrespectful to you. If they cut school, she will join them. If they smoke, drink, or take drugs, she will take up their habits. If they use four-letter words, her language will become coarse. Solomon warns his son, "Do not go along with them, do not set foot on their paths; for their feet rush into sin" (Prov. 1:15–16).

Watch as she and her friends approach the teenage years. Sometime between fourth and sixth grade, hormones begin to kick in. Girls approach or reach puberty. Boys get bigger and more aggressive. Boy-girl friendships become more serious. Bad habits, such as smoking and drug use, begin. Your daughters' friends begin to change, some not for the better. Friends who used to be safe company no longer are. If your daughter has good judgment, she will notice this herself and let them drift away; but if she doesn't, help her to recognize their bad influence and to give them up.

Discrimination is an especially good thing when it comes to your daughter's dates. If someone she's dating is a bad influence, do all you can to stop the relationship. Speak with her calmly about it. Compare his influence to biblical values. Assure her that you want what is best for her. Express your concern for him, but let her know that you don't approve of the relationship. Set limits on when and where they see one another. Let her see how much you love her; the more she is convinced of your love, the more she will find your views and limits reasonable and persuasive. And pray that the Holy Spirit would convict her of the need to avoid bad influences. Remember that you are protecting her, and sooner or later she will be glad you did.

Application *If you think a friend is a bad influence, limit the amount of time your daughter spends with that friend or only let her be with that friend at your house. Tell her that the reason you are not letting her spend the night or go over for parties is that you think her friend is not a good influence on her. Tell her how you see her friend influencing her in ways that are not good and that the more you see that kind of behavior in her, the less you'll want her to spend time with her friend. Assure her that you love her and want what is best for her.*

Bad Role Models

Consider the activities your daughter wants to be involved in. Where will a particular activity or program lead her? How have the older children in that group turned out? Would you want your daughter to be like them?

Evaluate not only the older children in the program but also the coach or group leader. The leader becomes a substitute parent and can have a strong influence on your child's attitudes and actions, both good and bad.

When one high school cheerleader developed anorexia, her counselor learned that her cheerleading coach continually told the girls that they weren't thin enough. In fact, several of the girls developed eating disorders. Look for adults who will reinforce the good characteristics you want your daughter to develop.

Don't assume that, because her friends or group leaders are in a Christian school or church group, she has the right companions. The cheerleading coach mentioned above was at a Christian school. Fifty-five percent of teens actively involved in evangelical churches reported having engaged in recent sexual behaviors, such as fondling and intercourse.[2] Even in a Christian environment, you need to know your daughter's friends and leaders.

Many parents worry that separating their daughters from bad friends or unhealthy activities will cause their daughters to rebel into something worse. The parents figure they will just let the friendships run their courses, or they hope their daughters will lose interest over time. Many parents and their children have come to grief this way. Yes, she will grumble; she may get angry; she may even defy you. Although she may not let you know it right away, however, she is glad you care enough about her to protect her. She doesn't always really want her own way, no matter what she says. Remember that discipline saves her soul (Prov. 19:18; 23:13–14). Do what is right, and pray for God to change her heart.

Teach Her to Keep Away from Bad Situations

You wouldn't leave a two year old at home alone or let a six year old bake cookies by herself. Good parents limit the risks and give a child responsibilities fit for her age, experience, and maturity. Just as a six year old, if left to bake by herself, can burn her hand in a hot oven, children left to handle situations for which they lack experience and wisdom can end up badly hurt. Think about your daughter's spiritual safety and teach her to recognize and avoid situations that could put her on the wrong path (see Prov. 1:15; 5:8; 7:6–27).

A bad situation is any set of circumstances that make it easier to sin.

Censorship Is a Good Thing

Physical food doesn't make a person spiritually unclean, but "thought food" influences the heart, out of which come "evil thoughts, murder, adultery, sexual immorality, theft, false testimony, slander" (Matt. 15:10–20; see also 5:21–22, 27–28). How we think influences how we act. And how we think is influenced by what we read, see, and hear.

Sexually explicit scenes incite lust. Seeing violence can harden the conscience. Illicit song lyrics play over and over in the brain, polluting one's thoughts. Encourage your daughter instead to read, see, and hear "whatever is true, whatever is noble, whatever is right, whatever is pure, whatever is lovely, whatever is admirable—if anything is excellent or praiseworthy"—so that she may think about those things (Phil. 4:8).

Curfews and Chaperones

"There's nothing good you need to do that you can't get done before eleven o'clock," said one father of teenagers. The later your daughter stays out, the fewer good things there are for her to do. Curfews protect your daughter from having too much idle time on her hands.

Knowing what evil lurks in the heart, previous generations sent along a responsible adult to oversee the meetings of the sexes. Situations didn't get out of hand with Grandmother looking on. Nowadays, individual dates are almost never chaperoned, and parties take place without adult supervision.

Don't be afraid to just say no: No, you can't go to that party. No, you can't sleep over at her house. No, you can't stay out later tonight. Don't be afraid to limit the range of your daughter's decisions. You want her to accept responsibility and achieve independence, but she shouldn't be given too much independence too soon.

Nip Budding Bad Habits

Habits develop through repetition into regular, nearly automatic patterns of behavior, and they can be good or bad. The Holy Spirit builds good habits of love, joy, peace, patience, kindness, goodness, faithfulness, humility, and self-control (Gal. 5:22–23). Against good habits there is no law, but bad habits are doing what the commandments forbid. The young are inclined to foolishness and the bad habits that result. You can't prevent your daughter's every bad action, but you can discourage bad actions from becoming habitual. Be on the lookout for the following patterns:

Self-indulgence. Self-indulgence leads to obvious bad habits such as laziness, drunkenness, drug abuse, and sexual immorality. A drug habit doesn't spring out of nowhere. Its roots lie in earlier habits of self-indulgence that were never broken. A child who learns patience, restraint, and self-discipline will have the control she needs in later years to just say no. Laziness indulged leads to more laziness, to making excuses (Prov. 22:13), to expecting something for nothing (20:4), and eventually to poverty (10:4–5). Children who learn to work hard when they are young will work hard when they are adults.

Complaining. Life isn't fair, and children know it—and complain. They also boast, quarrel, gossip, and say cruel things to one another. Speech is more than just words; it shows off the inner personality, and it also affects "the whole person" (James 3:5–6). Allowing your daughter to complain constantly will lead to her becoming more resentful and jealous. Allowing her to boast all the time will lead to her becoming even more proud. The more she gossips, the more she will dislike other people, and the more she quarrels, the more impatient she will become. She needs to learn self-control in her talk just as in her actions.

Harboring grudges. "I'll pay you back for what you did!" children say (see Prov. 20:22; 24:29). Because children like life to be fair, they also like revenge; they want to even the score. Harboring grudges, nursing envy, and cultivating pride lead to bitterness. Teach your daughter to forgive, to rejoice in the good things that happen to others, and not to think too much of herself (1 Cor. 13:4–8a). The family is the perfect laboratory for this, because sibling rivalry provides so many opportunities for hurt feelings, resentment, and jealousy—and for learning love.

Criticism. "Do not let any unwholesome talk come out of your mouths, but only what is helpful for building others up according to their needs" (Eph. 4:29). "Unwholesome talk" is more than just foul language; Paul contrasts it to "building others up." So then, whatever is vicious, untrue, mocking, quarrelsome, or derisive is unwholesome; it does bad and not good. "Reckless words pierce like a sword, but the tongue of the wise brings healing" (Prov. 12:18). "The lips of the righteous nourish many" (10:21). Keep a watch on how your daughter speaks to and about others. Teach her to nourish others with her words. "A word aptly spoken is like apples of gold in settings of silver" (25:11).

Cynicism. Like the one who sees the glass as half-empty, the cynic is pessimistic. She is bored and world-weary. Teenagers can declare just about everything "boring." They try their best not to be seen with their parents or at any activity they feel is beneath their dignity, such as a younger sister's birthday party. Don't allow your daughter to withdraw into her own superiority or to look on life as boring and meaningless. Show her how to perform good works and serve others with humility as Christ served us (John 13:1–17). If you notice pride and cynicism, pray for God to change her heart, and then help her focus on someone other than herself.

Disrespect. Disobedience and disrespect feed each other. If there are no consequences when your daughter disobeys you, she learns to disrespect you. But a daughter who has learned to obey her parents will also have learned to respect them, her teachers, and other authorities.

Will It Ever Stop?

Impatience, answering before listening, a quick temper, recklessness—the list of bad habits goes on and on. Until children are school age, it seems as if parenting is a nearly constant battle of breaking one bad habit after another. No sooner do you banish one bad behavior than another springs up. If you are diligent and consistent, however, this early work pays off, and for a while your daughter's behavior can seem almost self-sustaining. A tweak here, a fine-tuning there, and life at home is pleasant. But, like the evil spirit and the house "swept clean and put in order" (Luke 11:24–26), bad habits can come rushing back. Don't leave a vacuum that invites bad habits; continue teaching and encouraging good habits. Then, when she hits the teenage years, your daughter will be more cooperative and open to your guidance and the Holy Spirit's prompting.

In teenagers, as with toddlers, bad habits can spring up one after another. The cynicism you thought was gone comes back again. Just because she pronounced the boyfriend who mistreated her last year a loser doesn't mean she won't be attracted to him again this year. She may give up a friend who is a bad influence for a while and then become best buddies again. Just when you think she has become wise and responsible, she will do something to prove once again that she is still foolish.

Will it ever stop? Not completely, because she will always be a sinner. But if you are diligent, she will grow wiser, and as you nurture her relationship with God, the Holy Spirit will build within her good habits that last.

Teach Her to Apply God's Word to Everyday Life

The younger your daughter is, the easier it is for you to control her habits, situations, and companions. But as she grows older and gains more independence, she must make her own decisions. Every day your daughter will make choices without you standing by—whom to sit with at lunch; how to treat a teacher, a sister; what to do with her friends. "How can a young woman keep her way pure? By living according to your word" (Ps. 119:9 paraphrased).

But the Bible isn't arranged as a comprehensive flow chart; it doesn't lay out all possible situations, actions, and responses for each one of us to follow. Knowing how we should use any part of Scripture in a particular situation requires thought, knowledge, wisdom, discernment, and maturity (see 2 Tim. 2:15). Such qualities are just what the young lack. Your daughter may not recognize patterns in her experiences that parallel patterns in the Bible, or analogies between her experiences and what the Bible teaches.

For example, how should she apply the parable of the Good Samaritan? A Samaritan traveler came across a man who had been beaten, robbed, and left for dead. The Samaritan "went to him and bandaged his wounds, pouring on oil and wine," and took him to the innkeeper. Jesus said, "Go and do likewise" (Luke 10:25–37).

Ellie likes to ride her horse through the state park. If she comes across an injured man, how does she "do likewise"? Pour oil and wine onto his wounds before throwing him up onto the back of her horse? Then take him to a nearby motel and leave him with the front desk clerk? Or should she call 911 on her cellular phone?

To apply the Scriptures here, Ellie needs wisdom and some imagination. If the parable of the Good Samaritan had taken place today rather than two thousand years ago, how would this change the details of the story? What might the Samaritan use instead of oil and wine? Where would he take a man for medical attention? How would he travel? What do businessmen take on trips? If we came across such a victim today, what would be the best way to help him? Medicine and technology have changed, but the principle of the story has not. When Jesus says, "Go and do likewise," he isn't telling us to use wine and oil for first aid, but to show mercy to our neighbors (vv. 36–37).

To apply God's Word in her own life, your daughter needs to know three things: God's Word, the situation, and herself. To know what *she* should do, she needs to know how to apply *Scripture* to a particular *situation.*[3]

"Why won't you have sex with me?" a man who had recently become a Christian asked his date. "Because the seventh commandment says, 'You shall not commit adultery,' " she replied. "Well, so what," he countered; "neither of us is married, so it wouldn't be *adultery.*" One who is spiritually mature and knows the Scriptures knows that the seventh commandment regulates more than just the sexual lives of married couples. Every year *Playboy* goes to college campuses and recruits coeds to pose for the cameras. Should your daughter apply? Not if she understands the seventh commandment.

Train your daughter to look at the Bible with an inquiring mind: What were the people in the biblical situation doing? How did they understand their situation? How does that relate to my situation now? What are the differences? What are the similarities?

Help her to look at the world around her with biblical patterns in mind. Ask, Can you think of a person in the Bible who acted that way? Can you think of verses that describe that kind of attitude or action? When she needs to decide what to do, help her look in the Bible for patterns and analogies. When you tell her to do or not to do a certain thing, show her how the Bible relates to that decision. Teach her to look in the Scriptures to answer the question *What do I do now?*

Application *Teach your daughter to make decisions this way:* How should I apply the Scriptures to this particular situation? *Give her practice recognizing patterns and analogies. In family devotions, ask, If this story took place today, how would the details be different? Do we see people doing similar things today? Should we act the same or differently?*

Don't Forget Her Heart

"My son, give me your heart," the teacher in Proverbs says (23:26); "Write [my commands] on the tablets of your heart" (3:3; 7:3). As your daughter grows up, you will less often know what she is doing unless she tells you. Once the artificial controls of your supervision are removed, she will keep your teaching and God's law only if her heart is being changed by the inward grace of the Holy Spirit. With your teaching, training, supervision, and setting of limits, don't neglect your daughter's heart and her relationship with God.

Emphasize God's grace along with her obedience. Explain to her that we obey God because we respond to his love (1 John 4:7–5:5) and because he works in us both to will and to act according to his good purpose (Phil. 2:13; see also Ezek. 36:26–27). Remind her that he is loving and kind and will forgive her "seventy times seven," no matter how big the sin seems to her (see Matt. 18:21–22), and he will give her a clean heart (Ps. 51).

Teach her to confess her sins to God, and to trust in his forgiveness (1 John 1:9). "He who conceals his sins does not prosper, but whoever confesses and renounces them finds mercy. Blessed is the man who always fears the LORD, but he who hardens his heart falls into trouble" (Prov. 28:13–14). When you teach your daughter to come to God for mercy, you are helping keep her heart tender to the Holy Spirit so that her conscience will not become hardened.

When you make God's grace and forgiveness the centerpiece of your instruction about her Christian duty, you give your daughter hope that she will see the fruit of godliness grow. You teach her to enjoy God, to love him and delight in him. Out of this relationship comes her desire and ability to glorify him by the choices she makes and the way she lives.

Raising a daughter of good character requires balancing freedom and structure. You must provide enough structure to help her guard against sinful habits, situations, and companions, and yet allow enough freedom for her to develop and exercise the gifts God has given her and to grow to maturity in Christ. How can you know when to give her more freedom? When you see her heart being changed by the Holy Spirit, when you see that she fears God and trusts in his grace, you can trust her to make wise choices when you are not around.

For Further Thought and Discussion

1. Read Proverbs 13:20; Ecclesiastes 4:9–12; and 1 Corinthians 15:33. How do bad companions corrupt? How do good companions make us stronger? How will her friends influence your daughter?
2. Read Psalm 1; Proverbs 1:10–19; 7:6–23; and Philippians 4:8. What sorts of situations make it easier for us to sin? To resist sin? What situations might you need to protect your daughter from?
3. Read 1 Corinthians 13:1–13. What are the characteristics of love? Why is love so powerful? Why is it so necessary for family members to love each other? How can you teach your daughter to love others?
4. Read 2 Timothy 2:15. How can we be sure that we are applying the Scriptures properly?
5. Read Psalms 51:1–19; 103:1–18; Proverbs 28:13–14; and Matthew 18:21–26. How can we keep from hardening our hearts? How does the Holy Spirit keep us from hardening our hearts? How extensive is God's mercy and forgiveness? Why should God's grace be the centerpiece of teaching your daughter to obey God?

PART 4

Who Your Daughter Is

Points for Prayer

🌿 Pray that your daughter would thank God for making her wonderful.

🌿 Pray that your daughter would use her God-given abilities to glorify him and enjoy him forever.

"So God created man in his own image, in the image of God he created him; male and female he created them." —Genesis 1:27

CHAPTER 9

She Is the Image of God

"Who am I?" "Where am I going?" "What should I do?" "How do I fit in?" Growing up is a scary time for a girl. Between the ages of eleven and thirteen she goes through many changes—physically, intellectually, emotionally, and socially. Her friends' interests change from dolls and games to boys and dates, from running around the neighborhood and climbing trees to putting on make-up and going to dances. Boys treat her differently; she used to be a pal and a teammate, and now she is an object of desire and conquest. She used to be able to compete in sports with boys and win; now boys throw harder and hit a ball farther, and she's been kicked off the team.

Even her own body looks unfamiliar. Her comfortable world becomes uncomfortable. She knew that boys and girls were different, but she never realized *how* different. Boys seem to have gotten the better deal, and she thinks, *If this is what it means to be a woman, no thank you.*

Mary Pipher, a clinical psychologist, sees "confident, well-adjusted girls" transformed into "sad and angry failures" in the junior high school years. "Something dramatic happens to girls in early adolescence." Their "selves" disappear, their IQ scores fall, their math and science grades drop, they become less involved in activities and their families, they lose their confidence, and they become unhappy with their bodies. One of her teenage clients summed it up: "Everything good in me died in junior high."

Teenage girls are committing suicide, mutilating themselves, developing eating disorders, getting pregnant, using drugs, battling with their parents, and having trouble at school in unprecedented numbers and at earlier and earlier ages. Compared to just ten years ago, "girls are living in a whole new world."[1] Linda Bips, another clinical psychologist, says that she never used to prescribe medication for treating adolescents, but she now often considers that necessary because of the increased intensity of adolescents' psychological problems.[2]

Psychologists have tried to raise girls' self-esteem, and feminists have tried to empower them. But even the feminists agree that it hasn't worked: "If the feminist consciousness that developed in the sixties were going to have any effect on our daughters' behavior, it would be visible by now. It isn't."[3]

Why, after so many years, hasn't the women's movement helped our daughters feel better about themselves? Why are they in worse trouble than ever before? The feminist approach hasn't worked because it ignores what girls need most: to know God and themselves from God's perspective. To answer questions such as Am I worthwhile? What can I do? and What does being born a woman mean? a girl must start with the one who made her—God.

"Who Am I?"

Your daughter needs to know four things to have a proper self-understanding. She needs to know that she was created by God, that she was made in the image of God, that she was made a woman, and that she can become a "son" of God.

> **Application** *Teach your daughter the answers to these catechism questions:*
> *Who made you? God.*
> *What else did God make? God made everything.*
> *Why did God make you and everything else? For his own glory.*
> *How can you glorify God? By loving him and obeying his commands.*
> *Why should you glorify God? Because he made me and takes care of me.*[4]

She Is Not an Accident

Why don't we look like the alien characters in a Star Wars bar scene? It's just the way we evolved, say public schools, public television, and science fiction. Over billions of years, impersonal forces, chemical reactions, and gene mutations produced one life form after another until along came humans. We are just highly adaptive animals and an insignificant piece of a vast universe. Somewhere "out there" we're sure to find other intelligent life, some even better than we. After all, with a different series of random events, we *could have* turned out like any one of the Star Wars characters.

But the Bible says we are not here by accident. God made us: "So God created man in his own image, in the image of God he created him; male and female he created them" (Gen. 1:27). Indeed, God made everything—the earth and sky; the sun, moon, and stars; the plants and the animals; and last of all, people. Adam and Eve were the "crowning work of creation."[5] We didn't evolve from the animals (2:7). To know that your daughter was created is to understand that she is fearfully and wonderfully made and that she has a purpose and a responsibility.

She Is Wonderfully Made

God didn't make Adam and Eve, and then step back and let biology take its course. Each of us is made by God: "For you created my inmost being; you knit me together in my mother's womb. I praise you because I am fearfully and wonderfully made; your works are wonderful, I know that full well. . . . All the days ordained for me were written in your book before one of them came to be" (Ps. 139:13–14, 16).

The human body is amazing. The gracefulness of a dancer, the power of an athlete, the ability to write, and the simple act of picking up a dime are possible because of the bodies God has given us. Your daughter's heart beats and her lungs breathe in and out without her thinking about it. Her skin feels the sun and the wind, her nose smells baking bread and roses, her eyes respond to light, and her ears hear music.

The human mind is even more amazing. Our minds have been compared to computers, but even the best computers are still dumb machines—they do only what they are told. People have ideas, tell stories, invent new products, and think about God.

God made the particular person your daughter is. Whether she is dark-skinned or fair, whether she is short or tall, God made her just the way she is. He made her "wonderful." Our two older daughters who make the honor roll are wonderful, and so is our youngest who has Down syndrome—because God made them.

Most girls don't feel that their bodies or their abilities are "wonderful." They wish their noses were a different shape and their hair was a different color. Melissa hated being taller than all the boys in her high school; Sheryl hated being shorter than her younger sister. Just about every girl wishes she were someone else. Emphasize to your daughter that God made *her,* and he made her *wonderful.* She can be thankful for the way God made her.

Application *Teach your daughter the tenth commandment and that it means she shouldn't envy others but should be content with what God has given her and how he has made her.*

She Has a Purpose

Why did God make people? He made us for his own glory: to worship him; to give him honor, praise, and thanks; to love him and keep his commands; to take care of his creation and build his kingdom on earth.

"My daughter doesn't think she is good at anything," one mother said. This is common among teenage girls. Whatever your daughter's weaknesses, she will amplify them and forget about her strengths. But because God made her to glorify him, she is good at something.

A strong body is a gift from God. If she brings home stray kittens, God has given her a heart to care for his animals. If she organizes every child in the neighborhood to play her games, God has made her a leader. Whether she is the best baby-sitter in the neighborhood or she makes friends wherever she goes, each is a gift from God that he can use. Some of her most annoying qualities (to you) may be perfect for the job she will do. A child you can never get out of the house on time could become a missionary in a culture where "on time" is whenever you get there. A child who asks a million questions might discover the cure for a disease. God made her to fill a special place in his kingdom.

Your daughter is the only one just like her, but teenagers are often afraid to be different. They want to dress like everybody else and do the same things. Your daughter will feel the pull of peer pressure less if she realizes that being different is a good thing. She is not *supposed* to be just like everyone else, because God made her with the abilities that are right for her. Knowing this may also free her from the urge to be different in bizarre and sinful ways.

Most likely, she will not recognize her own talents. Ask ten people in your church what their spiritual gifts are, and at least nine will answer, "I don't know." It is easier to recognize others' gifts than to recognize our own. We don't think of our own abilities as being special; they come naturally to us, and we think, *Anyone can do that.*

Tell your daughter what you think her gifts and abilities are. Praise her when she does something well. Look for ways in which she can develop and use her abilities. Ellie has a way with horses; she has been riding since she was four. Sarah has a flair for the dramatic; she takes theater classes. Annie loves animals and babies; she feeds the cats and maybe she'll help in the church nursery when she is older. Ellie has a lot of confidence; she can lead any group. Sarah has tender feelings, but she also thinks about the way others are feeling. Annie gives great hugs and kisses and says, "I love you, Mom."

As you talk with your daughter about the things she does well, dream with her about her future. Help her to see beyond this year and the social problems that seem so big to her. Remind her that she was made to glorify God. Help her to think about herself in terms of how she can serve him, not how she compares to other people.

She Has a Responsibility to God

What your daughter does matters. One choice is not as good as another. She belongs to God. He made her, and he has the right to tell her what to do. Help your daughter to see that along with her gifts and abilities come responsibilities to her Creator.

A daughter who remembers that she belongs to God will make wiser choices. When should she have sex? When she is "mature enough to handle it"? When she "truly cares" for someone? Anytime, as long as she uses birth control? She has more to consider than her own desires, her parents' wishes, and society's standards. She recognizes that she must answer to the one who sees everything she does. She could deceive her parents, but she cannot hide anything from God. A wise daughter makes decisions based on her duty to God rather than on what her peers do.

She Is Not an Animal

Look in a mirror, and you will see your own reflection or image. The image is like you and yet not like you. "You exist on an entirely different level than does your image. The qualities belonging to your image in the mirror are but a reflection of your real qualities. So it is with God."[6]

We are not like God. He is self-existent; we were created. He is self-sufficient; we are dependent. He is infinite, eternal, and unchangeable in his being, wisdom, power, holiness, justice, goodness, and truth.[7] We are not. He is a Spirit and "does not have a body as we do."[8]

Yet we are like God, in a limited way, because he made us in his image. Although cartoons, Disney movies, and People for the Ethical Treatment of Animals have portrayed animals as just like us, we alone are the image of God.

She Is Like God in Being

Astro was the first pony Ellie ever rode. He belonged to the riding school, but Ellie loved him as if he were hers. When she had a scary fall off other school horses, she always went back to reliable, safe Astro. Soon after she got a pony of her own, Astro retired. He was in his thirties and no longer able to carry riders. The veterinarian kept him going for a while, but the day came when Astro was down, never to get up again. Ellie held his head in her lap, braided his mane, and cried. When he died, there was nothing we could say to her except, "He was a good pony." Animals have no soul that lives forever.

Because your daughter has a soul, she can know God. The most important thing about her is how she relates to God. In our society, girls easily become focused on their appearance: Am I too fat? Is my nose too big? Am I wearing the right clothes? Do I look like the models in *Seventeen?* You can help your daughter avoid this body image "crisis" if you remind her often that she is more than a body; she has a soul. She lives on every word that proceeds from the mouth of God (Matt. 4:4; Deut. 8:3). Her soul is what makes her most like God.

While she is more than a body, the body she has is good. More often than not, teenage girls say that they hate their bodies. Yet, our bodies are part of who we are. The whole person, that is, soul and body, is made in God's image.[9]

Your daughter's body is good because it reflects the image of God. Though God doesn't have a physical body, he is glorious and beautiful, and he made our bodies to reflect his glory. That glory "shines" in your daughter's body.[10]

Her body is good because it is what she needs "for the self-expression of the soul" and "to exercise dominion."[11] God is a Spirit, and he doesn't need arms to work, legs to walk, or eyes and ears to see and hear. We must see with our eyes, think with our brains, grasp with our hands, speak with our mouths, hug with our arms. By our bodies we do the work God gave us (Gen. 1:28–30; Matt. 28:18–20).

Application With your daughter, find out more about the human body and how it works. Discuss with her how wonderfully she was made, and talk about what she can do because of the body God gave her.

She Is Like God in Abilities

Why do people make laws and have judges? Why do they plant crops and build highways? Why do they invent new medicines and take apart atoms? Why do they read novels and play the piano? Why do *people* do these things while animals do not? Because people have abilities like God's. Although we have them in differing capacities, each person has a mind, strength, a conscience, the ability to make decisions, the capacity to love, and the ability to communicate that resemble God's.

Not only is your daughter good at something, but God made her like himself to represent and imitate him in the world. She can make beautiful things, solve problems, and discover ways to make life better for herself and others. She has a soul, a body, a will, an intellect, strength, and emotions.

At the same time, she must remember that God has qualities in a way she does not. Even some people are smarter than she is, some bodies are stronger or more attractive, and some abilities are more obvious and more valued. But "God is the great original,"[12] in whose image she was made to work and worship him.

> **Application** *In family devotions, discuss the character of God. Talk about how we are like and not like God, and how we are different from the animals.*

She Is Not a Man

For all the popularity of the book *Women Are from Venus, Men Are from Mars,* men and women really are in the same subset of God's creation: God made both in his image. "So God created man in his own image, in the image of God he created him; *male and female* he created them" (Gen. 1:27). Men and women are "basically persons."[13]

They have souls, bodies that are more alike than unlike, similar abilities, and will, intellect, and emotions. God gave authority over the earth to both man and woman (v. 28).[14] Both men and women work, build society, and take care of God's world. Women are not an alien species.

The truth is that men and women are both alike and different. A woman's body is like a man's and unlike a man's. God made people male and female so that together they could fill the earth with offspring (v. 28) and have oneness in marriage (2:24).

The differences between men and women go beyond biology. God also gave woman a different function in marriage. He made woman to help her husband (vv. 18–22). Adam and Eve were created to work together, but God made Adam the leader in the first family, and he made Eve Adam's helper.

A helper is not helpless. She is not weak, worthless, or incompetent. A helper assists, joins in, cooperates, supports, and lightens the load. A helper nurtures, inspires, comforts, encourages, and assures. A helper stands with and defends. A helper is a partner, a companion, a comrade, a colleague, an advisor, an advocate, a champion, a friend.

Woman is a helper in marriage. Like the excellent wife of Proverbs 31, she works hard; she can own a business and earn income. She advises her husband and becomes his best friend. She shares the responsibilities of running a household and raising a family. She eases his burdens by working alongside him. She is not like a parasitic vine that entwines the host plant and saps its nutrients. A wife is a complement who strengthens and supports her husband, as he strengthens and supports her. She encourages him on to greater love of God and good works, as he encourages her.

As a helper she is strong and talented but not in charge. The husband is the head of the wife (Eph. 5:22–33), not because she is inferior in abilities but because God appointed him.[15]

God made your daughter with talents and a purpose. He made her like himself, with glory and abilities like his own. He made her strong and competent to come alongside and share in the work of building God's kingdom. He made her a woman, and she can be thankful for that.

For Further Thought and Discussion

1. Read Genesis 1 and 2. How did God make man and woman? For what purpose? How did he make them "in his own image"? Why did he make them male and female? Why will it be impossible for your daughter to understand herself unless she first knows that God created her?

2. Read Psalm 139. In what ways are we "wonderful"? How should we respond to God our Creator? How should knowing that God created her influence what your daughter thinks, feels, and does?

3. Why can we be sure that God has given each of us talents and abilities? How can we discover our abilities? How should we use them? How can you help your daughter discover her abilities and then develop and use them? How should you respond if she says, "I'm not good at anything!"?
4. Read Genesis 1:27–31 and 2:18–25. How are men and women alike? How are they different? Why must a helper be strong and talented?
5. Read Proverbs 31:10–31. Describe the wife of noble character. How can you help your daughter grow to be like this?

Points for Prayer

❧ Pray that God would make your daughter a member of his family.

❧ Pray that God would renew your daughter in heart, mind, and actions.

"To all who received him, to those who believed in his name, he gave the right to become children of God." —John 1:12

CHAPTER 10

She Can Be a "Son" of God

It would be nice if we could leave the story with creation. But your daughter needs to know more about herself: she needs to know the bad news. God made man and woman "very good" (Gen. 1:31). In the Garden, they were holy and happy,[1] with "wisdom of mind, holiness of will, and good order of the affections, and all in harmony."[2]

And then they sinned (3:1–13).

Out of their first sin came all the sins and miseries of the world (vv. 14–19; Rom. 1:18–32)—death, disease, famine, earthquakes, birth defects, anger, murder, greed, injustice, tyranny, loneliness. Sin corrupted and distorted the image of God in man and woman. It broke their relationship with God and corrupted their relationships with each other.

The Image Is Marred

The *Titanic* was a beautiful and luxurious vessel the day it set sail. Now it lies wrecked on the ocean bottom. But we can still see some of its beauty and imagine what it looked like on its maiden voyage. It is, though not seaworthy, still a ship. It is still equipped with wooden decks, crystal chandeliers, and furnished staterooms.

We are still the image of God. In his mercy, God has kept us from being as bad as we could be. He restrains our sin, and he left us with diminished abilities so that we may recognize his glory, just as we can imagine from the wrecked and sunken *Titanic* the beautiful vessel it was. Yet, we lost the "good moral qualities of the soul."[3]

"The wages of sin is death" (Rom. 6:23; see also Gen. 2:17). Instead of knowing God, we are separated from him. Even more, we are his enemies. We lost the "supernatural gifts" of faith, righteousness, holiness, and salvation,[4] and we cannot be holy and happy. As we stand in ourselves, we can have no fellowship with God—only his anger and judgment. We are "sinners in the hands of an angry God." Our souls are spiritually dead.

Our bodies, too, are subject to illnesses, disorders, diseases, and death. Someone has said that from the moment we are born, we begin dying. Actually, death begins at conception (see Ps. 51:5). The seeds of cancers and heart disease lie in the genes. The effects of sin are built into our bodies. Not only that; our bodies age. Soon we need glasses and hearing aids and walkers. Eventually, we die.

In every part—soul and body; will, intellect, and emotions; gifts and abilities—we are infected with sin. We cannot do what is right and good. We hate God's law. We reverse right and wrong. We make errors, believe lies, and ignore the truth. We hate our neighbors and mistreat our friends.

Application *In family devotions, read the book of Romans. Ask, How does sin affect us? Does everyone sin? How can we have peace with God? Whom should we serve? What does it mean to live by the Spirit? How does a living sacrifice act?*

Relationships Are Harmed

The feminists are right: Marriage is a struggle for power; the sexes are at war. "Your desire will be for your husband, and he will rule over you" (Gen. 3:16). In addition to destroying our relationship with God, sin corrupted our relationships with each other.

The natural consequence of losing the holiness and happiness God gave us in creation is that we sin. We feel jealousy, anger, lust, greed, and hatred. We act selfishly. We think and say the wrong things. We misunderstand and take offense. We blame others and excuse ourselves. And so, it is only natural that we would have arguments, wars, loneliness, bitterness, murder, theft, fraud, rape, child abuse, and divorce.

In fact, God especially cursed the marriage relationship: the wife does not want to follow her husband's leadership,[5] and the husband does not exercise his leadership with love for his wife. Instead of experiencing unity in marriage, man and woman struggle against each other for domination and power. Sin infects the relationships between men and women.

We are lonely without God, and yet the human relationships we hope will fill the void break down as well. Sin has separated us from God and from each other. Even marriage, which God made for love, companionship, and help, has become a battle. We cannot have peace within ourselves, because we are full of sin; we cannot have peace with others, because we are full of sin; and we cannot have peace with God, because we are full of sin.

Your daughter should not be surprised, then, when she has problems, when she feels lonely, when she is frustrated by her lack of ability, when boys make crude suggestions, when her friends urge her to do wrong things, when her boyfriend dumps her, when bad things happen, when her world isn't perfect. She is seeing the effects of sin in the world, other people, and herself. Her problems won't go away if she is smarter or thinner or high or popular. Instead of becoming depressed or suicidal, instead of taking drugs or seeing if sex makes her feel better, instead of trying to look like a fashion model or doing anything to get a boyfriend, she should draw closer to God.

God shows us how far we have fallen with sin so that we will yearn for salvation and righteousness.[6] He wants us to look for the Savior he has provided, his son Jesus Christ. This is the good news.

She Can Become a "Son" of God

Image of God and son of God go together.[7] The bad news is that we ruined the image of God through sin. The good news is that Jesus renews the image of God in those who believe in him.

When your daughter believes in Jesus, she becomes a "son" of God: "To all who received him, to those who believed in his name, he gave the right to become children of God" (John 1:12). "Those who are led by the Spirit of God are sons of God. . . . you received the Spirit of sonship" (Rom. 8:14–15). When she believes, God adopts her into his family and makes her an heir with his Son Jesus (v. 17; Gal. 3:26–4:7).

Jesus Makes Her a Member of His Family

By an act of his grace, God transfers strangers into his family and gives them the benefits and privileges of sons. He gives us the name of "beloved sons," the status and dignity of sons, and the right to inherit grace, glory, eternal life—and himself. He gives us the right to call him Father and Jesus brother, and he gives us the Holy Spirit so that we recognize him as Father and act as his children should.

When your daughter becomes a "son" of God, she enters into an intimate, loving relationship with God. She experiences that great love that motivated the Father to send his Son Jesus to die for her (John 3:16; Rom. 5:8). That love draws her near, and she comes with confidence (Heb. 4:16), without fear of punishment (1 John 4:17–18), knowing that God cares for her (Luke 12:22–32; 1 Peter 5:7). Because God is the perfect Father, he is moved to tenderness and mercy by the pleas of his children (see Luke 15:11–24). He always forgives them and will never abandon them (Matt. 28:20; John 14:16–18; Heb. 13:5). Such love changes her, so that she loves God in return.

Adoption is part of the "unbreakable chain of events" of salvation. Once God decided to redeem us from sin, our calling, regeneration, justification, adoption, sanctification and perseverance in this life, and glorification in heaven became certain. When God adopts us into his family, he adopts us to make us good; he produces in us the character fitting for sons of God.[8]

This is good news for you and your daughter. You can trust that once God has begun a good work in your daughter, he will complete it (Phil. 1:6). When he adopts her into his family, he is promising that he will make her more and more holy, he will raise her up when she stumbles and guide her back when she strays, and he will bring her safely to heaven. You can entrust your daughter to God. Her sanctification doesn't depend on your doing everything correctly; it depends on God who is able to do all his holy will. When you pray for her to grow in grace, you are praying for what God has said he will do. So then, pray with confidence.

Jesus Renews Her in the Image of God

God has predestined his children to be conformed to the "likeness of his Son" (Rom. 8:29). We are made "new creation" (2 Cor. 5:17), "clothed" with Christ (Gal. 3:26–27), and "renewed" in the image of our Creator (Col. 3:10). Now we can be happy and holy.

When your daughter believes in Jesus, she will be conformed to that new life, because God is renewing in her all the good moral qualities she lost through sin: he is renewing her according to knowledge, righteousness, and holiness.

She is being renewed in heart (Ezek. 36:26–27). God himself gives her a "heart to know me" (Jer. 24:7) so that she will love him, trust him (Ps. 28:7), rejoice in him (33:21), fear him

(86:11), be thankful to him (111:1), pray to him (119:58), and want to obey him (v. 112). He gives her a broken and contrite heart when she sins, and a clean heart when she confesses her sins (51:10). He teaches her to treasure his Word in her heart (119:11) and to keep his commandments from her heart (Prov. 3:1). Even when her flesh and her heart fail, God is the strength of her heart (Ps. 73:26), because he has predestined her to be conformed to the image of Jesus.

She is being renewed in mind (1 Cor. 2:16; Col. 3:10). God gives her a new attitude (Eph. 4:23) about him, herself, sin, the world, and what she should do. He reveals who Jesus is (Matt. 16:13–17) and how great his love is (Eph. 3:19; 1 John 4:16). He gives her assurance of eternal life (2:3; 3:14; 5:13) and confidence that he hears and answers her prayers (5:15). He teaches her his ways (Ps. 25:4–5) and his law (119:125) so that she will have wisdom and understanding (Prov. 1:2). As her mind is renewed, she discerns God's will (Rom. 12:2), and by a growing knowledge of Jesus, she has everything she needs for "life and godliness" so that she can be effective and productive and make her calling sure (2 Peter 1:3–11).

She is being renewed in actions (Col. 3:1–17). As she is renewed in the image of God, she will walk as Jesus walked (1 John 2:6). Her new nature will become more and more evident by what she does. She will more often show compassion and kindness instead of malice and anger. She will have more self-control and forgive others more quickly. She will learn to be thankful in more situations and to do her work more and more for the Lord's glory. Through "the mysterious chemistry of the Holy Spirit,"[9] God works in her so that she wants to and actually does obey him (Phil. 2:13).

When your daughter believes in Jesus, God renews her in the image of Christ. She is set free from sin, the world, and the Devil to be what God created her to be, a woman made in his image. Because God is renewing her in his own image, she can fulfill her purpose of glorifying him.

Application *Teach your daughter that her salvation is an "unbreakable chain of events" and that God has predestined her to be conformed to the image of Jesus. Have her memorize Philippians 1:6 and 2:13: "Being confident of this, that he who began a good work in you will carry it on to completion until the day of Christ Jesus." "For it is God who is at work in you to will and to act according to his good purpose."*

Jesus Reverses the Effects of Sin

The good news of Jesus' coming was that he brought peace with God and the beginning of the kingdom of God. Now God begins to reverse the effects of sin as he renews his children in the image of Christ and sets them to work in his kingdom.

As God's kingdom fills the earth, as the church matures in its understanding of the Scriptures, as individuals grow in Christ, the knowledge of the Lord fills the earth (Isa. 11:9; Hab. 2:14). With the growth of the kingdom comes insight into the challenges of life. We lessen the pain from childbirth, cure cancers, revive heart attack victims, limit the damage from earthquakes, alleviate drought and famine, and spread the gospel. Men are learning to be better husbands, and women are learning to be better wives. It is a great time to have a daughter, because Jesus is removing the effects of sin, God's kingdom is growing, and the knowledge of the Lord is expanding.

Jesus Gives Her Equal Rights to His Kingdom

As God's kingdom unfolds, so do greater opportunities for women to be all that God designed them to be. The church is learning to use women's gifts in ministry, and cultures are giving women more opportunities to use their talents.

Because sin and its effects are still with us, men and women have a long way to go before they reach complete harmony. Husbands still dominate their wives, and wives still resist their husbands. Men treat women as inferiors, and women think men are oppressive. Men keep women from work God made them to do, and women step into work God didn't intend for them.

The battle of the sexes can be traced to the curse God placed on Eve's relationship with Adam because of their sin: "Your desire will be for your husband, and he will rule over you" (Gen. 3:16). A spin-off of that conflict is the tension your daughter will have with boys. They will tease her and hurt her feelings. She will misunderstand them and be angry. These boy-girl problems will intensify as she reaches puberty.

God cursed more than Eve's relationship with her husband; he also cursed her body: "I will greatly increase your pains in childbearing" (Gen. 3:16) or "your sorrow and your conception" (NKJV). Month after month and after the birth of every child the ceremonial law reminded women of this curse. When a woman had her menstrual period, she was unclean, and she had to make atonement and be purified eight days after her bleeding stopped (Lev. 15:19–30). After childbirth, she was unclean and excluded from the sanctuary for one to two months (12:1–8).

In college, my friends and I joked about these laws. My roommate called her menstrual periods "the curse." Sometimes, being a woman can feel like a curse.

The "Curse." Most girls start menstruation in junior high, and with it come the physical changes that attract boys and make girls feel awkward. Boys become bigger and stronger, and girls are suddenly losing the games they used to win. Girls' relationships with boys change off the playing field, too. Boys tease them about their bodies and try to brush against them in the hallways and lunch lines. They take them out on dates and hope for sex. Girls don't like some of this new sexual attention, and they certainly don't like the fact that boys are now physically stronger.

Not only does this new feminine body attract boys; it seems to repel parents, especially fathers. Lynn Johnston illustrated the dilemma of fathers and daughters in For Better or For Worse. As sixteen-year-old Elizabeth and her father sit on the sofa watching television, her father remembers how they used to cuddle when she was young. "I'd love to put my arm around her, but maybe she'd think it was wrong," he thinks. Meanwhile, Elizabeth wonders "why Daddy never hugs me anymore." When parents stop hugging their daughters, some girls may think, "Now that I am a sexual person, the only kind of physical contact I can have is sexual." And in fact, girls who menstruate at an earlier age are more likely to become sexually active earlier.

In addition to earlier sexual activity, early menstruation correlates to other social problems. The earlier girls hit puberty, the more likely they are to weigh more than other girls their age, be self-conscious, have poor body images, and develop eating disorders. They experience more problems in school and more depression. They are more likely to use drugs or abuse alcohol. They are more likely to become pregnant as teenagers.[10]

Early maturing girls aren't the only ones who experience problems, however. This is a critical period in any girl's development. Some girls hit puberty and spin off into depression, sexual promiscuity, and substance abuse. Many more lose their confidence, withdraw from their families, and become less involved in school and other activities. A majority of girls begin to hate their bodies—and themselves.

To come through adolescence still loving and serving God, your daughter needs more than preparation for the physical changes of puberty. She needs spiritual preparation as well. She needs to understand that Jesus redeemed us from the curse of the law (Gal. 3:13), and she needs to understand her role in God's kingdom.

Redeemed from the Curse. Like books without words for infants, the old covenant told the story of salvation in pictures and symbols. The laws about cleanness and uncleanness, sacrifices, and who could enter the sanctuary at what times pointed the Israelites to their coming Savior. The law was a guardian (Gal. 4:1–2), a supervisor (3:25), and a "tutor" (NASB) to lead God's baby sons to Christ (3:24).

Herod's temple reflected these laws in its architecture. It was built as a series of barriers. Gentiles were separated from the inner court by a wall. In the inner court, women were separated from men by another wall. Men were separated from the priests in the sanctuary, and only the high priest once a year could go into the innermost court of God's presence.[11] The temple and the law reminded all Israel of their sin, its curse, and their need for a Savior.

But now Jesus has "redeemed us from the curse of the law by becoming a curse for us" (Gal. 3:13). He took our sin and gave us his righteousness (2 Cor. 5:21; see also Rom. 8:1–4). He "destroyed the barrier . . . by abolishing in his flesh the law with its commandments and regulations" (Eph. 2:14–15). Now we *are* the temple of God (1 Cor. 6:19; Eph. 2:19–22; 1 Peter 2:5), and all believers are priests (1 Peter 2:5, 9) who can come at any time to God's throne of grace through prayer in Jesus' name (Heb. 4:16).

Jesus is the originator of "equal opportunity"—regardless of sex, race, or nationality, all believers become "sons" of God and inherit the kingdom of God. All are transformed into the image of Christ, the Son. Just as Jews and Gentiles share equally in the benefits and promises of Christ (Eph. 2:14–3:6), so do men and women: "There is neither Jew nor Greek, slave nor free, male nor female, for you are all one in Christ Jesus" (Gal. 3:28; see also 1 Cor. 12:12–13; Eph. 4:4–6). That means that in God's kingdom, your daughter is equal to boys.

Application *In family devotions, read the book of Galatians. Discuss how Jesus broke down the barriers between God and people. Ask, How would our lives be different if we lived in Old Testament times? What does it mean that Jesus became a curse for us? What does it mean when God calls you his son? How can you become more like Jesus?*

Equal to boys. Before puberty, girls see themselves as equal to boys. Girls find that society's expectations for them are pretty much the same as for boys. An athletic girl may even run faster and throw farther than boys the same age. Girls feel confident and proud to be girls.

Then their bodies change. And so do their attitudes about being female. A large part of the "crisis" of puberty for girls is the perception that, because they can no longer compete at arm wrestling, they are not as strong as boys mentally or emotionally either.

At the same time that your daughter may be delighted at her new maturity, she may also feel at a disadvantage. Counteract this by teaching her that she has the same relationship to God and to the world he created as boys do. She can still be a scientist or run for President, just as boys can. She is still being conformed to the image of Christ, just as boys are.

Assure your daughter that, even though her body is changing, *she* is still the same person. Whatever abilities she had before, she still has. If she was gifted at math in fifth grade, she is still gifted at math in eighth grade. If she was a good pitcher at age ten, she is still athletic at age fourteen. She is not changing into some strange and alien creature. She is simply maturing into the woman God intended she should be.

Even though your daughter has the same relationship to God and the world that boys do, she cannot simply ignore the fact that she is developing into a woman. She becomes a "son," but she is still God's daughter (2 Cor. 6:18). That is how God made her (Gen. 1:27).

God's daughter. "It's not fair that girls are not as strong as boys!" Ellie declared. She is very competitive, and she had a hard time accepting her arm wrestling losses in eighth grade. It would seem that men and women should be the same: they are both image of God; they both inherit the kingdom as "sons"; both are being conformed to the image of the Son Jesus. But men and women are different. Even though your daughter is equivalent to boys, she is not a boy.

To be content with how God made her, your daughter must be content *as a female*. She needs confidence that God made *her* wonderful.

While she is more than a body, her body is still part of who she is. And that body is female. God intended for her to grow and mature into a woman. Teach your daughter that her female body is wonderful. Reassure her about her appearance. (For ways to help your daughter like her body, see chapter 13.)

Although her female body is wonderful, the new sexual attention it attracts may not be. Boys are ruder, cruder, and more sexually graphic in their comments than they used to be. More than half of girls report that in school, boys touch them in ways they don't want to be touched.[12]

Your daughter can't change the boys in her school. Because of sin and our changing culture, boys *will* make her uncomfortable, no matter how many rules the school enacts against harassment. But as Ellie puts it, "Knowing that I am not a piece of meat does help." When your daughter knows that she is the image of God, a "son" of God, and made just the way God wants her to be, she will be better able to deal with the sexual attention she gets as her female body develops.

If your daughter focuses on her weaknesses, remind her that everyone has limitations. Not everyone *can* be a scientist. Not everyone *will* run for President. She will not be as strong as boys. She has to face up to it—she is never going to play in the National Football League. But neither will most boys. Remind her that she is in God's image, that God made her wonderful, and that he gave her the abilities that are exactly right for her. Remind her that the tenth commandment means that she should be content with how God has made her.

In addition to all the benefits of salvation and adoption, sonship has a particular, practical meaning for your daughter. Because Jesus redeemed us from the curse of the law, she can like herself as a female.

> **Application** *Girls who are athletic not only like their bodies more than other girls do, but they feel less intimidated by boys' comments and come-ons. They feel more confident, strong, and able to take care of themselves. Encourage your daughter to become involved in a sport. Consider giving her karate lessons.*

"I Am Somebody!"

"Repeat after me: 'I am somebody!' " is Jesse Jackson's trademark speech. Today's girls need a similar speech—anchored in the truths of Scripture. They need to be able to say with understanding that God made them and redeemed them. Given those realities, your daughter *is* somebody. God made her "wonderful." He gave her talents and a purpose. He made her in his own image. He renews her in the image of Christ so that she can serve and glorify him as she grows into a godly woman. This is biblical self-understanding.

Psychologists want our daughters to feel better about themselves. Christian parents want a daughter who loses herself in knowing and serving God. If she feels worthless, if she doesn't realize she has gifts, if she thinks she must have a boyfriend to be important, if she thinks being a woman is a handicap, if she is focused on her body, she won't be serving God. To be "somebody" as God intends, she needs to serve the Lord—and others—with gladness.

For Further Thought and Discussion

1. Read Genesis 3:14–19 and Romans 1:18–32. How did sin affect us and the world we live in? Should we ever be surprised when we have problems, trials, and sorrows? How does seeing the effects of sin make us long for God?

2. Read Romans 8. How does one become a son of God? What promises do God's sons have? How should God's sons live?

3. Read John 15:1–17; Philippians 2:12–13; and Colossians 3:1–17. How does God work in us? What does he produce? What is our responsibility? How do we "abide in Christ"?

4. Read Isaiah 11:1–9. How does the knowledge of the Lord fill the earth? Why don't we see the kind of peace described in these verses now; why do we still have problems?

5. Read Galatians 3:24–4:7; Ephesians 2:11–3:6; and 1 Peter 2:5, 9. How was the law a guardian and tutor? How did the ceremonial law point to Jesus? Why don't we keep the ceremonial law anymore? How are men and women equal in God's kingdom? How should this affect your daughter's self-understanding, her confidence, and her relationships with boys?

Points for Prayer

🌱 Pray that your daughter would learn to confess her sins to God and rest in his forgiveness.

🌱 Pray that your daughter would learn to serve others with a cheerful heart.

"Blessed [happy] are the people whose God is the Lord." —Psalm 144:15

CHAPTER 11

She Can Be Happy
Serving God and Others

Emotions reach higher peaks and lower valleys during the teen years than at any other age. One moment your daughter can conquer the world. The next her life is hopeless.

Today more and more teens seem unable to climb out of the valleys. They live in depression, dejection, embarrassment, moodiness, guilt, and self-hate. More parents are taking their daughters to therapy. More therapists are prescribing medication for teens' psychological problems. Self-mutilation and body piercing are new symptoms of inner turmoil. Even as parents, counselors, and teachers try to bolster girls' self-esteem, they seem more fragile and less happy than ever.

This is so partly because of the way girls think about themselves. But teaching your daughter that she is somebody because God made her and redeemed her is only part of keeping her from a self-image "crisis." What she does also affects how she feels about herself.

To overcome these "valley" emotions, your daughter needs to know why she feels unhappy with herself and what to do about it.

"Why Don't I Feel Better About Myself?"

Monica felt ugly. Cayenne felt guilty about fighting with her parents. Franchesca sat sullen and quiet in the therapist's office. Penelope tried twice to kill herself. Charlotte drank to "erase my life." Tammy couldn't go to sleep until she had cut herself with a razor. Rosemary worried about her appearance. Gail burned herself with cigarettes: "The next thing I knew I was burning my arm and it felt good. It felt clean."[1]

Why do girls despair or feel guilty, dirty, or ugly? The short answer to why girls don't feel better about themselves is sin. Guilt, depression, and dissatisfaction with ourselves are the inevitable results of sin. Sin means that there is actually something wrong with us. Because of sin, we have flaws and imperfections to feel bad about, and because of sin, we do things that make us ashamed and miserable. Sin gives us guilty consciences and makes us discontent (Rom. 2:14–15).

Parents, counselors, and teachers hope to make girls feel better about themselves by *telling them how good they are.* They don't use words such as *sinful, wrong,* and *bad* because these "lower self-esteem." But the problem with telling girls how good they are is that *they are not good*—and deep down they know it.

Like the girl with an eating disorder whose greatest fear was that someone would discover what a "fraud" she was, how "really nasty and mean" she was,[2] girls know they are selfish and disrespectful. They feel anger and helplessness, they give in to their passions, and they don't keep their promises. They do what their consciences tell them they shouldn't, and they fall short of their own goals for self-improvement.

Yet, as contradictory as it seems, your daughter can't feel better about herself until she feels *really bad* about herself, until she sees herself as a sinner.[3] The healthiest attitude your daughter can have is to see herself as a sinner.

When your daughter understands that she is a sinner, her understanding fits reality. She acknowledges that she was created for a noble purpose but has fallen far short of her high calling. She sees why the world is the way it is, why she doesn't do what she knows she should, why she fails time after time, and why she doesn't like herself. Most important, realizing that she is a sinner is the first step toward relief from her real problem, because only those who know they are sinners know they need a Savior (Matt. 9:12–13). Counselors and therapy methods and medications that simply ease the symptoms of depression and despair never touch this root of the problem.

She Is a Sinner

Girls with eating disorders were asked to fill in the blank in this sentence: "If I am not perfect, then I am _____." Most girls wrote in self-derogatory words such as "worthless," "inferior," "inadequate," or "stupid." And, the director of the clinic noted, they really meant it.[4] Girls who see themselves as "worthless" and "inadequate" actually are feeling the emotional effects of sin—guilt, depression, and mental anguish.

Paul wrote, "What a wretched man I am! Who will rescue me from this body of death?" (Rom. 7:24). Yet Paul continued, "Thanks be to God—through Jesus Christ our Lord!" (v. 25). None of us is able to be perfect; but believers are not left in despair.

You can teach your daughter that Jesus covered over our sin so that we are forgiven and at peace with God. He took the guilt of our sin so that we are free from punishment, and he appeased God's wrath so that God looks on us with favor. "Because of his great love for us, God, who is rich in mercy, . . . expressed . . . his kindness to us in Christ Jesus" (Eph. 2:4, 7), who died for us (Rom. 5:8). He gave us his perfect righteousness. Through him, sinners are made "holy in his sight, without blemish and free from accusation" (Col. 1:21–22).

To experience this release from the burden of her sin, your daughter needs only to repent and believe in Jesus. From the moment she first repents and trusts in Jesus, God declares her "justified"—"just as if I'd" never sinned *and* "just as if I'd" always obeyed. Sin no longer has control over her. When she has been justified, she can look at her imperfections and rejoice that Jesus has released her from condemnation. She can recognize her sins and thank God for forgiveness.

Application *Help your daughter understand God's forgiveness. Don't hold her mistakes and rebellions over her head or bring them up time after time. Assure her of your love and support, and when she confesses a sin, treat her as if you have forgotten she ever did it. Teach her that Jesus takes our sins and gives us his perfection. Pray that she would experience the joy of knowing she is a forgiven sinner. Have her memorize Romans 8:1: "Therefore, there is now no condemnation for those who are in Christ Jesus"; and 1 John 1:9: "If we confess our sins, he is faithful and just and will forgive us our sins and purify us from all unrighteousness."*

She Should Confess Her Sins

Although Jesus removes the guilt of her sin when she believes in him, your daughter is still a sinner, and she will sin (1 John 1:8). When she has done something wrong, she will feel guilty, ashamed, and "disturbed." In fact, the more your daughter sins and the more she keeps that sin hidden, the more dejected she will become. Eventually, she will lose the "joyful consciousness of forgiveness of sins and of favor with God."[5]

Unhappiness is a symptom of sin, but blessing and joy come from fellowship with God (Deut. 28:45–48; Ps. 32:1–5). So then, your daughter's day-to-day contentment depends on what she does after she sins. David describes this experience:

When I kept silent [about my sins], my bones wasted away through my groaning all day long. For day and night your hand was heavy upon me; my strength was sapped as in the heat of summer. Then I acknowledged my sin to you and did not cover up my iniquity. I said, "I will confess my transgressions to the LORD"—and you forgave the guilt of my sin. (Ps. 32:3–5)

David was miserable until he confessed his sins. Teach your daughter to confess her sins to God whenever she becomes aware of any thought, word, or deed that breaks God's law.[6]

Repentance is like breathing. To maintain physical life, we must get rid of carbon dioxide and inhale oxygen. In our spiritual lives we must confess sin and rely on the power of the Holy Spirit to obey God. We must turn away from sin and turn toward obedience to God. If we only empty our lungs but never breathe in, we soon pass out from lack of oxygen. Not only does your daughter need to learn to confess her sins to God; she needs to learn to obey him.

Her Primary Purpose

"This toy contains small parts. Not intended for use by children under age three." "Unleaded gasoline only." "Danger: Do not sit or stand. This is not a step." "Warranty does not include damages incurred from using this product for any purposes other than its intended use." To use anything safely, from a coffee pot to a ladder to a stuffed animal, it is important to know what the product was made to do and not to do. To be happy, your daughter must know what she was made to do—and then do it. She was made to glorify God and enjoy him forever.

Know God

God is the source of happiness and blessing, hope and confidence, goodness, power, wisdom, truth, and love. God bestows spiritual benefits (such as forgiveness and adoption) and psychological benefits (such as confidence, contentment, and hope). The emotional effects of sin (such as misery, dissatisfaction, despair, and guilt) are counteracted by the effects of knowing God. How can we be miserable when our sin is covered, our guilt is taken away, and God is looking on us with favor? Happy are they whose God is the Lord (Ps. 144:15).

Those who know God do the right things (1 John 5:1–3, 18) because God transforms them through the work of his indwelling Spirit. This transformation is the process of sanctification. God makes us actually holy, freeing us from the power of sin so that we want to do and actually do what is right.

Those who know God do the right things because they see what God himself is like. They recognize that he has the right to tell them what to do and that what he tells them to do is right and wise and for their own good. They remember that he sees everything they do and will judge them. They know that he hates sin and that Jesus paid the penalty for their sins by his sufferings. They give back to him thanks, offer themselves as "living sacrifices" (Rom. 12:1–2), and keep body and spirit holy out of reverence for God (2 Cor. 7:1). Knowledge and fear of the Lord motivate them to do the right things and be content with how God has made them and what circumstances he has put them in. Happy are those who fear the Lord (Prov. 28:14; see also Pss. 112; 128).

So then, the better your daughter knows God, the happier she will be. The better she knows God, the more confidence she will have in him, the more she will be able to resist peer pressure, the more self-control and emotional stability she will have, the more she will love others, and the more content she will be with what God has given her. Show your daughter what it means to trust his faithfulness, respect his holiness, look for his goodness, and depend on his grace.

Application *Watch for signs—such as despair, a casual view of sin, giving in to peer pressure, discontent, complaining—that signal that your daughter has a wrong idea about God. Show her from Scripture what God is like, and help her to see how that truth should change her actions or attitudes.*

Keep the Law

Automobiles are made to run on gasoline. We were made to "run" on the practices of "worship, law-keeping, truthfulness, honesty, discipline, self-control, and service to God and our fellows."[7] If we do not teach our daughters their Christian duties and responsibilities, we will help create unhappy girls who are bothered by guilty consciences, feel ugly, or burn themselves with cigarettes because they feel dirty.

Explain to your daughter that if she believes in Jesus, she has been declared holy, made a new creation, and called a child of God. "The old has gone, the new has come! All this is from God, who reconciled us to himself through Christ" (2 Cor. 5:17–18). "How great is the love the Father has lavished on us, that we should be called children of God! *And that is what we are!*" (1 John 3:1). Also teach her that now she must live as what she is. Remind her often, if she is one of his children, that God is at work in her so that she will want to and actually will do what is right (Phil. 2:13). A happy daughter asks, *What does God want me to do?*

Happiness comes through acting wisely (see Prov. 2–8), keeping the law (see Prov. 29:18; Pss. 1:1–3; 106:3; 112:1; 119:1–2), and accepting correction from the Lord (Job 5:17; Ps. 94:12). It also comes through counting others as greater than oneself, helping the weak and needy, and giving to others (Prov. 14:21; John 13:12–17; Acts 20:35).

Application *In family devotions, read the books of 1 John and James. Ask, How do we know we belong to God? How do we show our love for God? How do we show our love for others?*

Serve Others

The more time your daughter spends dwelling on herself, the worse she will feel. The more she thinks about herself, the more she will be embarrassed by her social faux pas, dissatisfied with her appearance, and convinced that she can't do anything right. When you see these symptoms, it's time to get her out of her bedroom and doing things for others.

Selfishness leads to unhappiness, but the Bible says that those who put others first (John 13:12–17) and are kind to the needy are happy (Prov. 14:21). Not only is serving others proof of loving God, but learning to serve others is a key ingredient of your daughter's contentment.

Serving Others Makes Her "the Greatest." A young man joined a mission organization expecting to do great things for God. Instead the mission assigned him to the headquarters maintenance crew, where he spent the next two years cleaning toilets. "Lord," he complained, "this is not what I signed up for!"

God's curriculum for greatness is learning humility, self-sacrifice, and service: "God opposes the proud but gives grace to the humble" (James 4:6). The one who loves his own life will lose it (John 12:25–26). "Whoever wants to become great among you must be your servant," Jesus said (Matt. 20:26). The young missionary learned that lesson in a very literal way: cleaning toilets prepared him to be a more effective evangelist.

Just like the disciples (see Matt. 20:20–28; Mark 9:33–35; Luke 22:24–27) and the young missionary, we all have trouble living out the principle of serving others. We naturally think more of ourselves and put our own interests first. Your daughter will be no exception.

I once introduced a Sunday school story by asking the children to imagine that there were two pieces of cake, one large and one small. "If you let your sister pick first, and she took the large piece, what would you do?" I asked. One child quickly responded, "Why would I let her choose first?" Because children are foolish, they are self-centered, selfish, and self-absorbed. They do not believe that "it is more blessed to give than to receive" (Acts 20:35).

Help your daughter to see that serving others is the mark of greatness. That is contrary to what the world teaches (see

Matt. 20:24–28; 23:5–12). Feminists in particular see service to others as demeaning—a sign of inferiority, victimization, or powerlessness. But when your daughter is serving others, she is being most like Jesus. Jesus "did not come to be served, but to serve . . ." (Matt. 20:28). He is the Servant (Isa. 42:1–9; 52:13–53:12; Matt. 12:18–21) who made himself nothing (Phil. 2:6–11) so that he might give us everything. He wrapped a towel around his waist, washed his disciples' feet, and said, "I have set you an example that you should do as I have done for you. . . . Now that you know these things, you will be blessed if you do them" (John 13:1–17).

"Becoming like Jesus" is a summary of the Christian's goal. Remind your daughter to "walk as Jesus did" (1 John 2:5–6) by adopting his attitude of humility and sacrifice (Phil. 2:5–11) and putting the good of her neighbor before her own desires (Rom. 15:1–3).

Serving Others Changes Her Attitude. Because children are foolish and self-absorbed, they are quick to see life as "unfair" when they don't get everything they want. Serving others helps your daughter put her own life in perspective. She may be glad she has hair of *any* color after working in a children's cancer ward. When she accompanies the church choir on her flute, her disappointment at being second chair in the school band may not feel so keen. Sorting clothes for a thrift shop, stocking the shelves of a food bank, or saving part of her allowance to buy diapers for the local crisis pregnancy center teaches her to think of others' physical needs. Helping the sick, the weak, or the needy teaches her to count her blessings of health, strength, food, and clothes.

Find ways that your daughter can help others. It is much harder to be dissatisfied with herself when she is thinking about what others need and how she can help them. Instead of dwelling on what she can't do or doesn't have, she becomes more focused on what she can give. There is satisfaction in discovering that she does have something to offer.

By Serving Others, She Discovers Her Talents. Most children don't really know what they want to be when they grow up. They don't know what they are good at doing or what they would enjoy doing as a career or a hobby. One way for your daughter to discover what she likes to do and is good at doing, is to help out at church, in her neighborhood, and at home.

Between the ages of eleven and thirteen, it is particularly important that your daughter recognize that she can do something well. By learning to serve others, she will be building the confidence she needs to be a useful member of God's kingdom. Because the road to contentment is paved with obedience and service, good parents will consider how they can stimulate their children to "love and good deeds" (Heb. 10:24).

"Finishing School"

As I stepped outside the airport, the city seemed almost foreign, and yet it was home. I had just returned from summer mission work in Lebanon and Pakistan, and I had brought back more than the *shalwar chemises*[8] in my suitcase. I had a new perspective. Even though I had lived outside the United States only a few weeks, I could see both the good and the bad in our culture more clearly.

Well-to-do parents used to send their daughters abroad to "finishing schools," where they would study cultures, learn the social graces, and come back ready to take up adult responsibilities. Such schools put the finishing touches on a young woman's education. Living, working, studying, or just touring in another country has made many happier and more fit for their Christian responsibilities, because it has changed their attitudes toward themselves and helped them evaluate the culture they live in.

Your daughter needs "finishing school" experiences, that is, she needs some fine adjustments to her attitudes about herself, others, and the culture she lives in. If you have the opportunity to travel with your daughter, so much the better; but you don't have to go to another country to impart the same benefits.

See society in light of the Bible. One of the immediate effects of travel is that we find ourselves immersed in another culture. We notice things we never thought about before, and sometimes that changes us. After mission work in Moscow a man said, "My attitude has changed from a focus on 'what am I getting?' to 'what can I give?' "[9] You can teach your daughter to "live like a foreigner" (see Heb. 11:8–10, 13–16; 1 Peter 2:11–12), to take a step back and really look at the society that surrounds her, and ask herself, *What is good and what is bad? What do I see that follows Scripture? What do I see that is contrary to Scripture? Why do we do things* this *way? Is this the way we* should *do them?*

Learn the difference between wants and needs. Christians who go to other countries commonly report a changed attitude toward material possessions. "Now things are not as important to me," said the man who goes to Russia every year. "People in Russia have so few things yet are able to enjoy themselves."[10] You can teach your daughter that she doesn't "need" everything she wants. Her happiness about what she has will depend on her attitude, not on the number of shoes in her closet. "Are we rich?" a girl asked her mother. "Well, we have everything we need, and a lot of the things we want," her mother replied. This mother is teaching her daughter to be content with the possessions she has.

See her purpose in life differently. Christians who go to other countries also commonly report seeing their purpose in life differently. A man who went to Korea as part of his military service decided to return there as a missionary. He preached the gospel, established libraries, and helped Korean villagers until he retired. You can teach your daughter to look for the needs of others and ask herself, *Has God given me the abilities to help that person?* Teach her that God has not given her abilities solely for her own benefit. Twelve-year-old Jamie just missed the role of Annie on Broadway, but she formed a group called Dream Kids. They sing for churches, nursing homes, and community groups, and all the money they earn goes to help chronically and terminally ill children. While it is important for your daughter to realize that she is good at something, that alone will not make her happy. Whether her abilities are great or small, true contentment comes through how she uses what she has.

Application *Have your daughter memorize 1 John 2:17: "The world and its desires pass away, but the man who does the will of God lives forever."*

Loving Parents Who Set Limits Have Happy Daughters

God is love (1 John 4:16). He demonstrates his love through Jesus (Rom. 5:8) and pours out his love into our hearts (v. 5). He surrounds us with his love (Ps. 32:10) and lavishes us with great love (1 John 3:1). God is loving, but he is not indulgent. Those whom the Lord loves, he disciplines (Prov. 3:11–12; Heb. 12:5–13). This is the kind of parents God calls us to be: loving parents who set limits. These parents have the happiest daughters.

Loving parents are patient and kind, they are not easily angered, and they don't treat their daughter rudely. They look out for her interests. They find joy in her accomplishments and rejoice as she grows in good character. They recognize that she has weaknesses, makes mistakes, and fails at times, but they don't berate her for it. They don't bring up everything that she has ever done wrong, but they forgive time after time without reminding her *how many* times it has been. They always protect, trust, hope, and persevere (1 Cor. 13:4–8).

Loving parents also discipline their daughter (Prov. 13:24), because they are not willing to be a party to her spiritual death

(19:18; 23:13–14). They take her spiritual interests to heart and nurture her in love and obedience to God. They teach her the practice of wisdom, and so set her on the path to blessing, health, honor, peace, safety, prosperity, a good name, favor with God and man—and happiness (Prov. 3–4).

For Further Thought and Discussion

1. Read Romans 7:14–8:4 and Galatians 3:22. In what ways are we "prisoners of sin"? How does Jesus set us free from sin? Why would knowing she is a forgiven sinner be the healthiest attitude your daughter could have?

2. Read 1 John 1:8–2:6. How often should we confess our sins? How do we deceive ourselves that we have not sinned? How could John say that we are all sinners and then demand that we walk as Jesus did? What hope do we have that we can obey God? Why do those who know God do the right things?

3. Read Matthew 22:34–40. How does loving God and neighbor fulfill the whole law? How can we show love for God? How can we show love for our neighbor?

4. Read Psalm 144:15. Why are those whose God is the Lord happy?

5. Think of the different ways families could combine levels of affection and control. How might the children in each of those families feel and act?

Points for Prayer

🎵 Pray that your daughter would have the true success of pleasing God.

🎵 Pray that God would lead your daughter into the right experiences and opportunities and prepare her for the things he wants her to do.

"The LORD . . . has filled him with the Spirit of God, with skill, ability and knowledge in all kinds of crafts. . . . He has filled them with skill to do all kinds of work. . . ." —Exodus 35:30–31, 35

CHAPTER 12

She Can Learn to Do Something Well

Rachel bypassed the period of rebellion that typifies so many teenagers. She didn't care about make-up and clothes. She was not swayed by peer pressure. Instead, everyone wanted to be like her. She didn't care what other people thought, and she didn't pick her friends only from the popular crowd. She was popular with her peers, but she wasn't afraid to be alone. Though not her school's most talented runner, through hard work she became the most successful distance runner, male or female, in the school's history. She entered the first class that included women at Virginia Military Institute and became a charter member of the VMI women's cross country team.[1]

At thirteen, Melissa was hanging out with the wrong crowd and getting into fights, and her grades were dropping. Her mother thought karate might teach her self-discipline. By age sixteen, while some in her old crowd had babies, she had earned a black belt and become a leader who wasn't afraid to say no when peers asked her to do something she didn't think she should. She was more outgoing, more involved in a variety of activities, and doing well in her school work.[2]

Twelve-year-old Lindsey is her father's favorite hunting

partner. He's a professional outdoorsman, and she has seen wilderness and wild life all across North America. In her closet, camouflage clothes hang next to designer jeans. She has learned that good things require preparation, patience, and persistence, and that some actions, once committed, can never be reversed. Her father hopes what she has learned in the outdoors has prepared her to make better choices when she becomes a teenager. She has a strong bond with her father, and already she is more apt to follow her own conscience than peer pressure. She told a potential boyfriend, "Oh, by the way, I like to hunt, and if you have a problem with that, we might as well. . . ." She also declared that she'd never marry a man who wouldn't eat the venison she brought home.[3]

Ashley's parents bought her a pony when she was ten. "Aren't horses expensive?" their neighbor asked. "Yes," Ashley's mother replied, "but it's cheaper than paying for drug rehab!" They had seen other people's daughters turn into troubled teens, and they hoped by giving Ashley responsibility for an animal and something to do after school, they could avoid similar problems and give her a chance to succeed at something she enjoyed. Four years later, their plan is working. Ashley is responsible, dependable, polite to adults, doing well in school, and jumping four-foot-high fences on a spirited thoroughbred.

Fourteen-year-old Christine has a beautiful smile and a beautiful voice and the poise to audition for stage roles, play opposite adults, or lead a room full of kindergartners in song. Thirteen-year-old Tammy helps her mother teach handicapped children during the summer. Sixteen-year-old Terri raises sheep for competition. Sejal volunteers at a nursing home. Sunni played the piano in church every Sunday from junior high until she left for college.

We hear so much about teens gone wrong that we can overlook the "success stories." Each of these girls and others like them are turning out well. So can your daughter.

Successful Girls

"There was just something different about her," teachers and peers say. Successful girls stand out from their peers, but they have a lot in common with each other. Though they excel in a variety of ways, all the girls who flourish share similar characteristics and experiences.[4]

Independence from Peers

Successful girls go through their teenage years more independent of their peers than do other girls. Like the others, they want to be popular, but they are not willing to do just anything to have it. When they believe their friends want them to do something that is actually bad for them, they don't go along just to fit in. They have a strong sense of who they are and where they are going, and they stand up to peer pressure. They try to make the right moral choices, even if this means their peers reject them. In fact, they often feel isolated and lonely.

Successful girls spend a lot of time by themselves, but they also have a few well-chosen friends they really trust. They don't pick their friends based on who is most popular, whose parents make the most money, or who is the best-looking and best-dressed. They don't join groups that have reputations for bad habits such as drug abuse or sexual activity. They are friendly with people outside their own cliques, and they don't ridicule others or spread gossip. They help others because they can imagine how someone else feels.

How important is popularity to your daughter? When she feels lonely or left out, help her to look beyond her limited experience and focus on the future. Remind her that if she does what she knows is right, she will never regret it and that the small choices she makes today will make a big difference years from now. Tell her that when her classmates make bad choices (such as not studying, or using alcohol or drugs) they are limiting what they will be able to do in the future. Encourage her that God has a good future for her (see Jer. 29:11).

Urge her to choose her friends wisely. Look for activities where she can acquire wholesome friends who share her interests. Even one friend who shares her values means she does not have to stand alone (see Eccl. 4:9–12).

A Higher Goal

Successful girls have higher goals than popularity. They have an idea of what they want to do with their lives, and they make choices based on long-term goals. They have the self-control to refuse drugs and sexual encounters. They feel that their lives have a purpose and that they can contribute something to others. They are not self-absorbed, and they have a belief in something that is larger than their own lives and problems. They get involved in a higher cause that sustains them and gives them a wider perspective than their immediate situation.

Remind your daughter that as a Christian, not only should she have higher, long-term, heavenly goals, but she has God himself. She has God's Word to tell her what is right and warn her about what is wrong. She has the power of the Holy Spirit to convict her of sin and give her the desire and strength to obey God. She has fellowship with God to sustain her when she is lonely or troubled.

Adults Who Care

Successful girls have a strong bond with adults, especially their parents. Even in adolescence, they stay close to their families, and they recognize that their parents really do love them. They identify with adults, and they have at least one adult who encourages them to work for high goals. Their families and other groups such as church provide a safe haven in which to grow, develop their abilities, and learn responsibility.

To form a strong bond with your daughter, talk with her, listen to her, and play with her. Show interest in what interests her. Encourage her, praise what she does well, and gently help her improve where she is weak. Spend time with just her. Let her know that she can always come to you, and when she really needs you, let her interrupt what you are doing. Pray for her and with her.

Look for other adults who can be friends, role models, or mentors to your daughter. The more connected she feels to adults, the less she will be influenced by her peers. At times, she may be more open to suggestions from her coach, the youth group leader, or her best friend's mother than from you. Build a network of adults who will echo and reinforce the values you yourself are teaching her.

Confidence Through Competence

Girls who learn to do something well go through the transition years from childhood to adulthood with more confidence. They stay involved in the activities that interested them as elementary students, and their skills give them a feeling of continuity between childhood and adulthood. They are not embarrassed to work hard in school or excel in sports or other activities, and they blossom into successful adults.

When girls develop specific, practical skills, they also learn more general skills such as cooperating with others, handling both success and failure, accepting responsibility, and practicing self-discipline. They are less likely to be shy and more likely to feel that they can handle their problems. They are less concerned about their appearance. They become leaders and then reach back to help others.

While your daughter will feel better about herself if she learns to do something well, remember that most children, by definition, have average, ordinary talents. Your daughter doesn't have to be the fastest runner or a piano virtuoso to be successful. *Every* child can be successful, because true success is walking in God's ways, and that results from the right relationship with God.

True Success

The world measures success by how many trophies one wins or how much money one makes or how famous one becomes, but true success is being pleasing to God. A daughter who has the right relationship with God abides in Jesus (John 15:1–17), and like a tree planted by a stream, she prospers and bears fruit (Ps. 1:3). Success results from God being with us (see Josh. 1:5–9; see also Gen. 39:3, 23) and producing in us characteristics that please him, such as the following:

- fearing and obeying God (Prov. 3:7–8; 9:10–12)
- respecting parents (13:1)
- acting wisely (3:13–17; 8:32–36)
- being generous (11:25; 25:21–22) and honest (11:1, 3; 24:23–25)
- avoiding sexual sin (5:1–23; 6:20–7:27)
- not thinking too highly of ourselves (18:12)
- working diligently (6:6–15; 13:4; 28:19)
- responding to discipline (13:13, 18; 29:1) and instruction (16:20)
- avoiding bad companions (1:10–19)
- choosing friends' wisely (22:24)
- helping the needy (31:8–9, 20)
- being careful in what we say (12:13; 13:3; 18:13)
- not hardening our hearts but confessing our sins (28:13–14)
- using our abilities for work (Gen. 1:28–30; Ex. 35:30–36:2) and ministry (1 Cor. 12)

Your daughter will walk in God's ways as she abides in him, but she will not be perfect. Even successful girls still do some foolish things. At times your daughter will feel unhappy and seem out of control, but God does not go on hiatus while she is a teenager. He continues his work of conforming her to the image of Jesus. When your daughter entrusts herself to God, he will make her prosper.

Help Your Daughter Develop Her Talents

Just as a human body needs its arms, eyes, feet, fingers, lungs, and every other body part, the church needs your daughter and the gifts God has given her (see 1 Cor. 12:7–27). God wants your daughter to develop spiritually, physically, mentally, socially, and emotionally so that she will be truly fit for the work he wants her to do. Help her discover and develop her abilities so that she grows into a competent worker in God's kingdom.

Most girls have a poor sense of their strengths and abilities. They don't know what they want to do or should do with their lives. They have an inflated sense of their weaknesses, especially during the junior high years.

Pray that God would show you the talents he has given your daughter and guide you in developing them. Pray that he would lead her into the right experiences and opportunities and give her an interest in the things he wants her to learn. Then expose her to a wide range of activities, skills, groups, and individuals. Assume that she is interested in everything and can learn to do just about anything until she proves otherwise. Within reason, if you can afford the time and money for an activity and she wants to do it, give it a try. Some of her gifts will surprise you.

Allow Her to Take Responsibility

Letting go of our little girls terrifies us parents. There are times I can't imagine giving my daughters the freedoms my parents gave me when I was sixteen or eighteen. I'm not looking forward to the day Ellie gets her driver's license or Sarah goes off to college. Yet the best way to ensure that our girls *won't* be ready for life on their own is to shield them from responsibility now.

When we parents prevent children from taking responsibility or making decisions, we mean well. We want to avoid the messes and mistakes that may result. We want to keep them safe.

We want to feel a part of their lives as they grow up. But if we are always hovering, rescuing them, criticizing their ideas, and taking over their projects, we don't teach them to be competent and take responsibility for their own actions and choices.[5]

On the other hand, good parents don't expose their daughters to genuine danger or just let them do whatever they want. Fortunately, parents are not reduced to an either-or, all-or-nothing position. You can give your daughter some independence without at the same time abandoning her to her own foolishness.

Let her make choices within boundaries appropriate to her age, maturity, and experience. Give her choices within a subset of choices. As she matures in wisdom, enlarge the boundaries.

Help her think through the logical consequences of her options. Listen to her ideas and ask questions such as "What do you think will happen if you do that? Is that what you want to happen?" "Is that what the Bible teaches you to do?" "What other choices will you have if you do that?" "What problems could you have? How would you solve them?"

Let her solve some of her own problems. If she comes to you for advice, don't give her a detailed plan; instead, ask questions such as "What do you think you should do now?" "Will that make your problem better or worse?" "What does the Bible say we should do when things like this happen?"

Resist the urge to rescue her. Let her make *some* mistakes. Don't shield her from *all* the consequences of her bad decisions or irresponsibility. But never compromise her safety!

Find a place where she can be the expert. Give your daughter independence within a safety net. Ellie knows more about horses than we do, but she still has a trainer who keeps an eye on her at the barn. Backstage, Sarah is supervised, but she must put on her stage make-up, take care of her costumes, and listen for her entrance cues. Lindsey lands fish nearly as big as she is, while her father looks on. Each of them has an area where she can feel like an expert, exercise some independence, and use and test her decision-making skills.

As you enlarge your daughter's boundaries, let her know that you are trusting her to make the right decisions and that you are always available to give her advice and help. Then pray that she *would* make the right decisions and that God would keep her from harm.

Application *What kinds of responsibilities and decisions fit your daughter's age, maturity, and experience? List some ways you can give her responsibility, and then give her some.*

Ask Questions

Your daughter has strengths. Look for what she enjoys and what she does well. Is she an avid reader or does she always want to be outdoors? Can she make you laugh and does she sense when others need cheering up? Does she draw in the margins of her notebooks? Does she finish her homework without your reminding her? Does she introduce herself to adults and make friends wherever she goes? Do others want to do what she does, while she herself goes her own way?[6]

Ask your daughter what she enjoys and what she wants to do when she grows up. Look for adults who are doing what she is interested in. What kind of preparation did they have for their jobs? How did they end up in their line of work? Look for someone who can advise your daughter or serve as a mentor.[7]

Ask other adults who know her well—relatives, her school teachers and guidance counselors, your pastor or youth group leader, her Sunday school teacher, her coach or group leader, a summer employer, a neighbor, her best friend's parents— what they think she does well. You won't see all that she does or have the expertise to judge all her talents. Does she have a promising career in science? Is she really that good a singer? Will her hook shot get her a college scholarship? Can she succeed at that big university? Get some advice from people who have more experience than you do.

Teach Her Your Own Skills

Once they are no longer playing at it, most children find chores pretty boring. They don't beg to do chores the way they beg to play soccer. Yet, the most natural way to develop your daughter's talents is to teach her to cook meals, sew on a button, change a flat tire, do laundry, mow the grass, and clean the kitchen floor. Doing chores well is not a glamorous accomplishment, but she will like the feeling that she can take care of herself and handle a variety of tasks. And she needs those skills anyway. After all, she won't live with you forever.

Get Involved in Her Education

Like chores, school is an opportunity to reveal and develop our children's abilities—an opportunity they often don't appreciate. School is fun at first, but when it comes to the hard work, children would rather play. Yet, solid achievement in school prepares your daughter for work as an adult. School work exposes her to different disciplines and gives her a foundation of knowledge and skills she will need no matter what she grows up to do. Her report card reveals her strengths and weaknesses, but don't look at just her grades; take particular note of what she enjoys. If she makes As in math, but hates it, she probably isn't going to be a mathematician.

Give Her a Wide Range of Experiences

Ellie let us know what she wanted to do when she was four years old. We live on the edge of a state park with horseback riding trails. One day a rider came by and stopped to let Ellie pet the horse, and the only way John could get her away was to promise that when she was five, she could ride a horse. Ellie fell in love with horses that day and has never wavered. But most children don't discover what they want to do or focus on one passion at such a young age. Sarah dabbled in this and that until she found theater.

Most likely, your daughter will not discover her talents with the first thing she tries. Besides, she has more than one talent, and God has more than one thing for her to do in his king-dom. Since she won't know she is good at something unless she tries it, look for opportunities to give her a wide range of experiences. Children are naturally curious and interested in just about everything.

Sports. Girls involved in sports are generally happier and more confident. They find friends who share their interests, and they have more adults involved in their lives. They learn self-discipline, how to work toward a goal, and that sacrificing short-term pleasure can bring long-term gain. They learn to handle both winning and losing. They have something to occupy their time after school or over a long summer. They are less likely to be sexually active as teens.[8] They have a healthy way to relax and relieve stress. Girls in sports are less concerned about their appearance than are other girls. They like their bodies for what they can do with them. Because they are more active, they have healthier appetites, healthier body weight, stronger muscles, and more endurance.

Creative arts. Because she is made in the image of God, your daughter has some creative talent. She might be good at playing an instrument, singing, dancing, photography, writing, sculpting, weaving, drawing, or some other of the creative arts. Like sports, the arts are beneficial whether your daughter turns professional or remains strictly amateur. She can make friends who share her interests, and she can develop close relationships with adults. The arts require her to practice and thus teach her self-discipline and working toward a goal. They give her something to occupy her time now and a hobby to enjoy all her life. They help her express her feelings, relax, and relieve stress. The arts lift her spirits and stimulate her thinking. They draw her to the beauty and truth of God and teach her to give him thanks for the good things he has given her to enjoy.

Service to others. Volunteers are happy people. They are less cynical, less depressed, and less self-absorbed. They concentrate more on the needs of others than on their own needs.

They feel that they have a purpose, and they believe that they can make a real difference in another person's life and even the world. They meet interesting people and interact with adults. They learn to count their own blessings of health, family, and possessions. They learn responsibility and grow in love for others. Thirteen-year-old Sara and her mother worked for a year at a soup kitchen, and her mother thought the experience came at the perfect time. Instead of getting caught up in her seventh-grade peer culture, Sara made friends with people of all ages. She became especially fond of the older people there, and they helped her learn to draw, played card games with her, and told her stories about their lives. At the same time, she saw firsthand the unattractive consequences of abusing drugs and alcohol. And she learned that she could make a difference: she could give hungry people food and sad people companionship.[9]

Work skills. Early work experience, such as delivering newspapers or baby-sitting, is another indicator of adult success. It develops good work habits such as being on time, not goofing off, being able to follow directions and solve problems, cooperating with others, being flexible, and not complaining. It can teach your daughter responsibility, gives her opportunities to form relationships with adults, and keeps her busy and out of trouble. Real work experience helps her find out what she actually does and doesn't enjoy.

Light a Fire

Education is not the filling of a pail, but the lighting of a fire, said poet William Butler Yeats. In exposing your daughter to different activities, you are not looking just to fill up her time or her head. You are looking to ignite her God-given abilities.

Try to find an activity that lights a fire within your daughter, something she enjoys and shows a talent for. Then help her learn to do that well. It may be something you were interested in, and it may be something totally unexpected. It may even be something you don't think girls are usually interested in.

Eleven-year-old Sara competes in soap box derbies, sixteen-year-old Terri raises sheep, and twelve-year-old Lindsey fishes and hunts. Remember that each of us is different. God gave your daughter the abilities that are right for the work he wants her to do.

As you expose her to different activities and consider the skills she is developing, remember that she fits into God's overall plan that the world increase in the knowledge of the Lord (Isa. 11:9) and the whole church grow to maturity in Christ (Eph. 4:12–15). Her academic strengths, her athletic abilities, her creative talents, her gifts for service, her work skills, and even the hobbies she enjoys blend into the perfect set of talents to fulfill God's plan (see Ps. 139:5, 13–16; Gal. 1:15). Every ability she has is a "spiritual gift," because God gave her each of them to equip her for "the common good" (1 Cor. 12:7).

Application *Ask your daughter what she is interested in learning. Then look for some activities that fit her interests, the time you have available, and the money you can afford to spend. Schools, community colleges, camps, and summer recreation programs offer a variety of sports, creative arts, and special interest classes. In addition, there are organizations, clubs, and private instructors for just about every interest and activity. Don't worry if she changes her mind after a few weeks or months; try something else, until you find the thing that lights her fire.*

Rejoice in Her Growing Maturity

Teenagers are both scary and delightful. Unfortunately, we usually focus on the scary parts. We read about underage drinking, car accidents, and teenage pregnancy, and we overlook the true joy that parents of teenagers have: seeing their children's abilities blossom, observing their accomplishments, and watching them maturing into useful adults.

When our children are babies, we sit up nights rocking them and wondering what they will be like when they are bigger. In their teen years, we begin to see their potential realized. As your daughter becomes good at something, the path God has ordained for her comes into clearer focus.

Rejoice as you see your daughter's talents developing. Thank God for her growing maturity and usefulness in his kingdom.

For Further Thought and Discussion

1. Read Exodus 35:30–36:3; Romans 12:3–21; 1 Corinthians 12:4–14:39; Ephesians 4:11–16; and 1 Peter 4:8–11, and list the gifts and abilities God gives. What other abilities does God give? How can the use of these gifts increase the knowledge of the Lord in the world and help the church grow to maturity?

2. How would you answer someone who says, "I'm not good at anything!"? How could that person discover her abilities?

3. Read Isaiah 11:9; Psalm 139:13–16; 1 Corinthians 12:7; and Ephesians 4:12–15. Why is it important that your daughter learn to do something well?

4. Read Joshua 1:5–9; Psalm 1; and Proverbs 3:7–18, 33–35. What is success? What characterizes a successful daughter?

5. How much independence should children have?

6. What do you find most scary about your daughter growing up? What do you find most delightful?

Points for Prayer

🌹 Pray that your daughter would learn at an early age to value her character over her appearance.

🌹 Pray that your daughter would be a good steward of the body God has given her.

"I praise you because I am fearfully and wonderfully made;
your works are wonderful, I know that full well." —Psalm 139:14

C H A P T E R   1 3

She Can Like Her Body

Aimee Mullins holds world records in the 100- and 200-meter dashes, as well as the long jump. She is the co-founder of HOPE—Helping Other People Excel—a nonprofit organization that helps disabled athletes receive training. She has appeared in *Sports Illustrated* and *Esquire* magazines and modeled for the House of Givenchy. And, like a spider, she has eight legs—that is, four different pairs of artificial limbs. Her legs were amputated just below the knee when she was a year old.

Yet Aimee wears minidresses and shorts and seems entirely comfortable with her body. She stops to let children touch her metallic sprinting legs and entertains friends without her prostheses on. She realizes that many people feel uncomfortable around her, but she hopes they will like her for who she is inside. "I feel perfectly normal, and I've never had legs," she says. "The truth is, I'm sort of lucky to have this body, because it forced me to find my strength and beauty within."[1]

Cayenne played soccer and didn't worry much about her appearance, until she reached junior high. When her body changed with puberty, she felt that her hips and thighs were flabby and her hair was the wrong color. She became self-conscious about her clothes and uncomfortable with boys' teasing. She thought every other girl in her school was prettier than she was.[2]

More girls are like Cayenne than like Aimee. Aimee is unusual, not because she has artificial legs, but because she likes her body.

"I Hate My Body!"

By age thirteen more than half of girls are unhappy with their bodies. By age seventeen, four out of five girls dislike their bodies. Women of all ages are more likely than men to rate themselves as physically unattractive. Models complain about their "thunder thighs." "I'm so fat. I'm so ugly," girls write in their diaries. "I'm a pimply whale," fifteen-year-old Monica said of herself; "when I walk down the halls I feel like a monster." "Let's face it," said fifteen-year-old Cayenne, "I'm a dog."[3]

"The body is at the heart of the crisis of confidence" that hits girls during the junior high years, says Joan Jacobs Brumberg.[4] As their bodies change in size, shape, and hormonal balance, adolescent girls become preoccupied with how they look. They compare themselves to the beauties in movies and magazines—and hate what they see in their mirrors.

Why do so many girls hate their bodies? There are physical, cultural, and spiritual reasons, but the roots of all these factors go back to the Fall.

Envy, Shame, and Imperfection

Eve reached out and took the forbidden fruit because she was not content with having all the trees in the Garden but one, and she wanted to be "like God" (Gen. 3:1–6). But as soon as Adam and Eve ate the fruit, they felt ashamed of their naked bodies. They were no longer comfortable with themselves, with each other, or with God (vv. 7–10). In addition, their bodies began to show the effects of sin and death (vv. 16–19).

Envy, discontent, and shame are still at the heart of modern-day dissatisfaction with our bodies. Girls look at each other and the pictures in magazines and wish they could be as tall or thin or pretty as that one is. They feel ashamed of their noses, hair, or hips. They strive for a "perfect" body, but because of the Fall our bodies are not perfectible. We are born with body flaws. We are subject to illness, diseases, and disorders, and then we make it all worse by the things we do or don't do.

When a teenage girl looks in the mirror and hates what she sees, she is exhibiting the symptoms of sin. The sin in her heart makes her ashamed and envious. Her attitude is the product of sin; but her body itself is imperfect because of sin, and she is growing up in a sin-infected culture. This is why physical factors such as earlier puberty and social influences such as the media and her peers can contribute to her "body crisis."

Earlier Puberty

"I feel like Alice in Wonderland," twelve-year-old Stacy said about the way her body changed so quickly with adolescence. Between the ages of eight and ten, girls begin to show signs of sexual development. Then, in just two to four years, girls almost double their weight, their body fat increases 120 percent, their breasts develop, they grow several inches, and their angular bodies become curvy.[5] These new bodies don't look quite right to them. Rosemary hated the way her wiry body "turned to dough" with puberty.[6]

Through infancy and childhood, girls and boys have similar growth patterns. Then, about two years before boys do, girls experience a dramatic growth spurt. In a culture in which even models and beauty queens think they are overweight, this growth spurt is a problem. Although they need body fat and skeletal growth, especially in the hips, for menstruation to begin, girls (and sometimes their parents) interpret the physical changes of puberty as becoming "fat."

This metamorphosis occurs three to four years earlier than it used to. Girls look mature at twelve or thirteen, but they still think like children. Because twelve- and thirteen-year-old girls don't have the cognitive and emotional maturity to match their developing bodies, they are less able to handle the sexual attention that results and more vulnerable to cultural messages and pressures.[7]

Cultural Influences

What is a "normal" body? How your daughter answers that question depends largely on how much she and her peers have been influenced by advertising, magazines, and movie stars. Models and beauty queens are thinner than they used to be, and the standard they set can't be achieved just by being healthy. In 1950 the White Rock mineral water girl was 5'4" and weighed 140 pounds. In the 1990s, a 5'7", 128-pound beauty contestant had to lose fourteen pounds, eat only three egg whites for breakfast, work out at a gym three hours a day, and have cosmetic surgery to increase her bust size.[8] And at the same time that girls are absorbing our culture's emphasis on youth and beauty, they are less connected to their parents and other adults who could give them a more realistic perspective.

"My Body Is Me"

Imagine your daughter digging up the potatoes, when her trowel hits with a *clink* something buried in the ground. Curious, she digs further and discovers a beautifully decorated, sealed ceramic jar. She brushes the dirt off the outside, washes the jar, and puts it on the window sill in her room—but never opens it. What a shame that would be! The real treasure is inside.

This is what girls are doing with themselves. They are cleaning up their outside and ignoring the real treasure inside, their souls. Ask an adolescent girl today, How can you make yourself a better person? and she will likely list a series of "body projects," such as losing weight or buying new clothes. She answers the questions Who am I? and Who do I want to be? in terms of her physical appearance.[9] Girls think about their bodies almost continually. They stare into full-length mirrors and weigh themselves every day. Girls hope to solve their emotional or social problems by losing weight, getting new make-up, or coloring their hair. An anorexic thinks if she can be thin enough, she will be a good person. She reduces her whole life to her body.

But the Bible teaches the opposite: "As water reflects a face, so a man's *heart* reflects the man" (Prov. 27:19). While her body is part of who she is, and it reflects the image of God and enables her to think and work and pray, the most important thing about your daughter is not how she looks, but how she relates to God. Like a clay jar containing a treasure (see 2 Cor. 4:7), her body serves an important purpose, but her real value comes from what is inside. It is not what she eats but what comes out of her heart that matters most (Matt. 15:1–20). So then, your daughter must learn to put her character above her appearance.

We can't do anything about our daughters' reaching puberty at younger ages, but we can address their spiritual needs and counteract the cultural influences that make them unhappy with their bodies. By teaching your daughter what the Bible says about her body and her relationship to God and by giving her practical ways to resist cultural pressures, you can help her like the body God has given her.

Teach Your Daughter What the Bible Says About Her Body

Your daughter needs to understand that she consists of two parts, a body and a soul. Her body is "dust," but it contains a soul that will last forever (Gen. 2:7; Ps. 103:14; Eccl. 12:7).

Her Body Is a Clay Jar
The words that most commonly describe our physical bodies in Scripture are "dust" and "clay." The Lord God formed the first human body from the "dust of the ground" (Gen. 2:7), and like a potter who molds the clay, he still forms each person

as he pleases (Job 10:9; Isa. 64:8; see also Isa. 29:16; 45:9–13; Jer. 18:1–6; Rom. 9:20–29). But, like clay, our bodies are weak and fragile; our bodies are dust and will return to dust (Gen. 3:19; Job 4:19–21; Ps. 103:14; Jer. 19:11).

God Is the Potter. God gave your daughter's physical body its own kind of splendor (1 Cor. 15:40). He made her wonderful (Ps. 139:14), giving her strength, glory, and abilities after his own image. He gave her the body that is right for her and for the work he wants her to do in his kingdom.

To be content, then, your daughter must first acknowledge that her sovereign Creator made her body. He knit her together in the womb for his own good purposes (Ps. 139:13–16). He gave her eyes, skin, and hair of a particular color. He decided whether she would be tall and how many freckles would pop out on her nose from the sun. He planned for Sarah to be a strawberry blonde and for Annie to have an extra chromosome. When your daughter grumbles about her body, she is grumbling against God. Teach her to be thankful, even for her imperfections (see 2 Cor. 4:7, 16–18; 11:30; 12:7–10), because they come from God.

Her Body Is Dust. Your daughter's wonderful body is "wasting away" (2 Cor. 4:16). Her youth will pass and her beauty will fade (Prov. 31:30; Eccl. 12:1–7). Her body will age, and someday she will die (Job 4:19–21). If she thinks her body is the essential "her," growing old will bring her bitterness and frustration. But if she develops good character, she can look forward to the future (Prov. 31:10, 25, 30).

This may be a hard lesson to get across to your daughter, because, right now, she can't imagine growing really old. She can't imagine getting wrinkles or gray hair. In a culture of face lifts and hair coloring, youth can seem perpetual, especially to the young. The wise daughter learns that she cannot preserve her body (Ps. 22:29). Impress upon your daughter that her soul, not her body, should be her primary "project."

Her physical body is only temporary (1 Cor. 15:35–58; 2 Cor. 5:1–8; Phil. 3:20–21), but it is the vehicle and container for her soul, which will live forever. This is why her relationship to God is more important than her appearance and her character than her dress size. "How much greater is the glory of that which lasts," Paul wrote (2 Cor. 3:11). No part of her body can equal the priceless treasure of knowing Jesus and inheriting his kingdom (Matt. 5:29–30; 13:44–46; Phil. 3:7–11).

Application *Teach your daughter that her body is a "clay jar," that her real treasure is the character that results from her relationship with God. Have her memorize Proverbs 27:19: "As water reflects a face, so a man's heart reflects the man."*

Her Body Can Be a Temple of God

Sin in her heart, her body, and the culture around her explains why a girl hates her own body, but Jesus reverses the effects of sin when your daughter believes in him. He gives her a new heart, and he also makes her body his dwelling place, a temple of the Holy Spirit who lives in her and gives new life to her body (1 Cor. 6:19; see also Rom. 8:10–11).

By living in her, God gives glory, dignity, and splendor to her body. Though her body is dust, it becomes a holy temple (1 Cor. 3:16–17), a holy sacrifice (Rom. 12:1), a "holy instrument dedicated to God's service."[10] Because God makes it his temple, she can like her body.

But this liking of her body can only go so far. It is still only a "house of clay," an "earthly tent" (Job 4:19–21; 2 Cor. 5:1–5). Like the tabernacle the Israelites carried with them in the desert, her current body is only a temporary dwelling for the Holy Spirit, who is a "deposit, guaranteeing what is to come" (2 Cor. 5:5). Your daughter's natural body has only an earthly splendor, and it will be replaced by the heavenly dwelling, the spiritual body (1 Cor. 15:40–44; 2 Cor. 5:1–5). Though her body carries the life of Jesus, it also carries the death that comes from sin; it will still age and someday die. Her salvation is not complete until Jesus changes her mortal body into a body that will never die.

Explain to your daughter that though her body will waste away, inwardly she is being transformed into the likeness of Jesus, and someday, even her body will be transformed into a glorious, heavenly, spiritual body (1 Cor. 15:42–58; 2 Cor. 4:16–5:10; Phil. 3:20–21). Pray that, while she is still young, she would understand that after her body dies, her soul will stand before God. And pray that she would trust in her Creator and Savior (Eccl. 12:1–7; Heb. 9:27).

Application *Teach your daughter that her body is a temple of the Holy Spirit but an "earthly tent." Have her memorize Philippians 3:20–21: "But our citizenship is in heaven. And we eagerly await a Savior from there, the Lord Jesus Christ, who, by the power that enables him to bring everything under his control, will transform our lowly bodies so that they will be like his glorious body."*

Help Your Daughter Like Her Body

Most girls have normal bodies, yet they don't feel normal. Aimee Mullins had a rare and disfiguring birth defect, yet she feels normal. It's not how your daughter looks but how she thinks of herself that determines whether she feels normal or grotesque. Aimee could have hidden herself away from the world, but instead she helps others because she learned to be comfortable with herself. She is not embarrassed by her body. She knows that the most important part of herself is the person inside.

Girls who don't like their own bodies make bad choices: about what and how much to eat, how they act around their friends and peers, what they are willing to do to be popular, the boys they date, and whether they engage in sexual sin. There is a connection between how girls feel about their bodies and what they do with them. When you help your daughter like her own body, you prepare her to make better choices and become a more effective member of God's kingdom.

Your daughter's body is not the most important part of her, but it *is* part of her. Even if it were possible in today's culture to ignore her appearance, she can't simply do that. In order to be content with the body God has given her so that she can serve and glorify him in her body (see 1 Cor. 6:19–20 NASB), she needs some practical help.

Emphasize a Healthy Body

The body your daughter has is a gift from God. When you teach your daughter a healthy attitude toward her body, not only are you teaching her to like her body; you are also teaching her to respect the gifts of God and to be a good steward of what he has given her. She gets only one body in this life. Help her learn to take care of it.

A balanced diet. About 20 percent of teenage girls develop eating disorders, but another 25 percent of children are medically overweight. Neither is healthy. Girls with eating disorders are malnourished, vulnerable to infections, and at risk for heart attacks. Overweight women have higher rates of breast and other cancers, are more likely to have a child with birth defects, and have increased risks of stroke, diabetes, and other diseases. Girls who eat a balanced diet in moderation will avoid the extremes of being either overweight or too thin.

> **Application** Get a copy of the USDA food pyramid, which gives guidelines for good nutrition. Talk with your daughter about why her body needs these different foods.

Exercise. Our grandmothers were right when they told us to eat our vegetables and go outside and play. Girls who participate in sports burn more calories than their peers, have better muscle tone, feel stronger, eat healthier meals, and have more endurance. And they feel better about their bodies. Look for activities that will help your daughter develop a strong body but in which girls of different shapes and sizes participate and feel welcome.

Realistic standards. Even though she is healthy, your daughter may not like her body. Advertising and movie images are powerful influences on how modern society defines beauty.[11] By age five, children pick pictures of thin people as "good-looking." Our eyes have been trained to think the ideal woman should be tall and thin, but today's models and actresses are actually well below what medical professionals consider a normal, healthy weight. Point out that women come in different shapes and sizes. You can't say too often that models and actresses aren't typical and some of them aren't even healthy.

Application *Visit an art museum or the local library with your daughter. Look at paintings and sculptures, and compare those women to the photographs in today's fashion magazines. Talk about how today's movies and magazines have influenced our idea of beauty. If your daughter complains that she is "fat," help her determine if that is a realistic assessment of her weight. Look up her age, height, and weight on an insurance chart or a pediatrician's graph, or calculate her Body Mass Index (BMI) by multiplying her weight by 703 and dividing that number by her height in inches two times. (A healthy, relatively lean teenage girl has a BMI of 21 or 22, and she is not "overweight" until her BMI is 25 or higher.) Have her memorize Psalm 139:14: "I praise you because I am fearfully and wonderfully made; your works are wonderful, I know that full well."*

Watch What You Say

Remember that girls at this age reason emotionally and are going through a self-conscious stage. Your daughter can feel that there is something wrong with her even if she is developing normally and has a strong, healthy body. She may find her sudden growth spurt embarrassing and thus misunderstand off-hand remarks or take jokes seriously. Until she reaches puberty, she likes it when you to notice that she is getting bigger; now she could think getting bigger is a problem just when she should be doubling her weight.

Don't tease her about how much she eats. Don't show alarm at how fast she is outgrowing her clothes. She will be sure you just said, "You're fat!"

One day I was making cupcakes for Annie to take to school. "You're my little cupcake," I said to Ellie. "Thanks a lot!" she pouted. "What's wrong?" I asked. She replied, "You think I eat too much! You called me a cupcake because you think I eat too many of them." When I explained that I meant it as a term of endearment, she laughed at herself; but her first reaction showed her insecurity.

Give your daughter compliments; praise her inner qualities; tell her that you like the way she is growing up. Point out the things she can do now that she is older, such as lift heavier things, swim faster, or reach a glass in the top cabinet without a stool. Let your daughter know that you admire the young woman she is maturing into. As her body changes, reassure her that she is normal. Tell her that bodies come in different shapes and sizes and each body develops at its own pace. Remind her that she can't change the rate at which her body is growing (see Matt. 6:27).

Lessen Her Body Exposure

Mirrors became common in American middle-class homes at the end of the nineteenth century. Home scales became common in the 1920s. These conveniences provided girls with opportunities to scrutinize their own bodies as never before.[12] At the same time, changing fashions were revealing more of the female body to the scrutiny of others. Since then, hem lines have gone up, come down, and then gone up even more. In comparison to previous generations, today's girls have more body exposure than ever.

Hide the mirror. Part of this body overexposure is easy to fix.

One mother simply got rid of the scales and has no full-length mirror in the house. Don't provide your daughter opportunities to catalog her imperfections for hours on end in the privacy of the bathroom or her bedroom. The less she studies her body in the mirror and the less often she weighs herself, the more likely she is to be satisfied with her appearance and weight.

Add fashion common sense. Although marketing research is showing greater tolerance among teens for body differences,[13] your daughter's peers can be very cruel, and she doesn't have to be atypical to feel self-conscious. The right colors and styles of clothes, a good haircut, or some strategically applied cosmetics can make a difference. Dark-colored clothes will make her appear smaller; vertical stripes will make her look taller; collars will pull attention to her face. Help her pick clothes that look good on her. Remember to give her compliments.

Address the sexual factor. The "right clothes" for a teenage girl can reveal a lot of her body and attract attention from boys. Fashions popular with teenagers reflect a culture that sees sexual expression and displaying the body as a "critical personal right."[14] Since the sexual revolution, many parents have become neutral about their teenagers and sexuality, but this is not an option for Christian parents. Teach your daughter that the seventh commandment influences how she dresses. Explain to her that what she wears affects the way other people, especially boys, think of her and treat her. Explain that she should not lead another person to stumble into the sin of sexual fantasies (Matt. 5:27–30; 1 Cor. 10:23–11:1). Emphasize that, if she is a Christian, her body is the temple of the Holy Spirit (1 Cor. 6:19) and that she is God's ambassador (2 Cor. 5:20). Exercise veto power over what she buys and what she wears in public.

Application *Have your daughter memorize 1 Corinthians 6:19–20: "Do you not know that your body is a temple of the Holy Spirit, who is in you, whom you have received from God? You are not your own; you were bought at a price. Therefore honor God with your body."*

Lessen Peer Pressure

Your daughter's peers are a powerful force in her life. She cares what they think, and her peers think thin people are the prettiest, the smartest, and the most worthwhile. They critique each other's make-up and clothes. They talk about their diets at lunch time. Girls have to have the right look to be accepted.

Your daughter's peers get their values from the mass media. They may talk to their parents a few minutes a day, but they watch hours of television. They listen to the radio and watch music videos. They read teen magazines and follow the lives of movie stars. To counteract this media-influenced peer pressure, your daughter needs adult support and supervision.

Stay close. Parents are the most important adults in a girl's life. Talk to her about growing up, making choices, and last weekend's football game. Talk about what her friends say and do, and help her keep her peers' ideas and teasing in perspective. Compliment her and tell her how much you admire her. Play with her and laugh with her and hug her. Girls whose parents hug them and hold them feel better about their bodies and themselves.[15]

Open some "protective umbrellas." One of the differences between girls today and girls one hundred years ago is that the "protective umbrella" has folded up. Activities, societies, and clubs for adolescent girls that provide "intergenerational mentoring" by adult women are dwindling.[16] At precisely the time that they should be getting more support and protection from adults, adolescent girls in our society get less. Look for activities that give your daughter opportunities to get to know older women. Grandmothers, coaches, neighbors, her Sunday school teacher, the Girl Scout leader, and her best friend's mother are wonderful resources. Don't waste them.

Emphasize Character

The "protective umbrella" had two purposes: to keep adolescent girls busy enough to stay out of trouble and to help them develop self-control, service to others, and belief in God. Parents used to emphasize good works instead of good looks because they were wise enough to realize that real beauty comes from within (1 Peter 3:3–6).

Self-control offers obvious physical benefits, such as exercising consistently or not getting fat from overeating. It also affects how a girl feels about her body, because one of the results of sinning—including the sin of lack of self-control—is self-hatred. The result of self-control, however, is doing and thinking what is right.

Serving others helps a girl like her own body more, because she spends less time thinking about herself and contemplating her own flaws and imperfections. The more she thinks about others and how she can help them, the less she will be dissatisfied with herself.

Belief in God is the most important and indispensable ingredient, because he produces the other ingredients of self-control and love for others. He reverses the effects of sin and gives a girl's body dignity and splendor by living in her. He gives her confidence, contentment, and hope. He renews her mind and heart. He produces the character that makes her beautiful.

Teach your daughter that she makes herself beautiful by doing what is right (1 Peter 3:4–6). Wisdom gives her the "unfading beauty" of goodness, knowledge, self-control, perseverance, godliness, kindness, and love (see Prov. 1:8–9; 3:21–22; 4:9; 2 Peter 1:3–9). No matter how beautiful she is on the outside, without wisdom and good character, she will not be attractive, to God, to others, or to herself (Prov. 3:3–4; 11:22).

Compliment your daughter for her inner beauty as she grows in wisdom. Get her out serving others. Spur her on to greater knowledge and love of God. Self-control, service to others, and belief in God are the ingredients of good character—and of a healthier body image.

The Perfection Trap

Stacey was the perfect daughter: an honor student, elected to the student council, a talented singer and dancer, involved in her local church, a volunteer at the local nursing home, and pretty enough to finish as the runner-up for Miss America. But beneath her perfect exterior lay a debilitating spiritual condition.

"Unless my school work, activities, relationships, and appearance were perfect, I was not only unhappy, but I was also broken, depressed and in complete turmoil." She found it hard to forgive others, and she continually felt guilty over her own mistakes. She knew that she was a child of God, but she struggled to believe that with God's forgiveness she could "start over with a clean slate." Her inner struggles brought her to the brink of anorexia. She received help, and then began trying to help other women. Since then, she has met "countless anorexics and bulimics who know with their heads that Jesus loves them, but their hearts are thoroughly unconvinced."[17]

Girls with eating disorders are trying to alleviate a true spiritual dilemma: a guilty conscience. They know they fall short, and they recognize that unless they are perfect, they are worthless, even condemned.

Eating disorders are on the increase among young teenage girls who hate their bodies and themselves, but it is only one of the more obvious manifestations of this spiritual dilemma. Maybe your daughter is trying so hard to be the perfect daughter, the perfect student, the perfect Christian, that she has killed all her enjoyment of God. She may be so focused on duty, that she is struggling with a load of guilt, despair, and self-loathing as she sees herself fall short time after time. She may think she must persevere in her Christian walk through her own strength. She may even be trying to earn her salvation.

There is only one way out of the perfection trap: to understand that Jesus took her sins and gave her his perfection, and that not only did Jesus die for her sins on the cross, but he obeyed the Father perfectly in her place. When God looks at your believing daughter, he chooses to see Jesus' perfection instead of her sin. Yes, she must be perfect to enjoy God's favor

(Matt. 5:19–20; James 2:10), but in Jesus she *is* perfect (Eph. 1:3–6; Col. 1:21–22).

Look for symptoms that your daughter is in a perfection trap. Fear of making a mistake, fear of admitting her mistakes, overwhelming embarrassment, reluctance to forgive others, a belief that she has to earn God's love through obedience, fear that you won't love her if she tells you what she has done wrong, struggling to accept God's forgiveness after confessing a sin, and self-loathing could be warning signs of an eating disorder, but they are definitely signs that she needs to understand God's salvation better.

If your daughter has not been born again, tell her continually about the free gift of God in Jesus Christ. If your daughter is a believer, whenever you teach her about her Christian duty to obey God, always emphasize the following truths: She cannot earn God's favor; she has that already in Jesus. God always forgives her and loves her no matter how often she falls; he loved her and chose her when she was his *enemy*. She does not obey out of her own strength; strength comes from abiding in Jesus. She will grow in good character as God works in her, and he will never stop working in her until she is made perfect, body and soul, in heaven.

For Further Thought and Discussion

1. Read 1 Samuel 2:8 and Psalms 103:1–18; 113:4–7. How does God "raise us from the dust"? What kind of dignity does he give us?

2. Read 2 Corinthians 5:1–10 and Hebrews 11:8–10. In what ways do we live in a "tent"?

3. Read 2 Corinthians 3:4–6:2; 12:7–10; 13:4. In what ways is our inner life more important than our outer appearance? How does God transform our weakness into strength?

4. What attitude should we have about our physical bodies?

5. How do self-control, service to others, and belief in God (or the lack of them) show character? Why is belief in God essential for good character? For contentment with one's body?

6. Read Matthew 5:19–20; Ephesians 1:3–5; Colossians 1:21–22; and James 1:10. Do we have to be perfect? Can we be? How can the perfection trap rob a believer of the enjoyment of God? Why is it important for your daughter to understand that she is not perfect but Jesus is?

PART 5

Sex, Dating, and Marriage

Points for Prayer

❧ Pray that God would develop the fruit of self-control in your daughter.

❧ Pray that God would give you a close relationship with your daughter.

"It is God's will that you should be sanctified: that you should avoid sexual immorality; that each of you should learn to control his own body in a way that is holy and honorable, not in passionate lust like the heathen, who do not know God. . . . For God did not call us to be impure, but to live a holy life." —1 Thessalonians 4:3–5, 7

C H A P T E R   1 4

She Must Develop Sexual Self-Control

One of the foremost reasons it's scary for parents to think about their daughter growing up is s-e-x. Will she engage in sexual activity before she is married? Will she get pregnant? Can we trust this boy she just walked out the door with? Can we trust *her* to exercise good judgment and self-control?

Parents are right to fear that their teenage daughters will engage in sexual activity before marriage. It's statistically more likely than other teenage hazards. Only 10 or 11 percent of teens take illegal drugs. About 20 percent use alcohol. Fifteen percent of teens will have an automobile accident. But one out of two girls have had sexual intercourse by age eighteen.[1]

In 1998, the Centers for Disease Control reported that, for the first time in a decade, more than half of high school students surveyed said that they had never had sexual intercourse.[2] Groups such as Best Friends are helping girls say no to sex, the federal government is paying for abstinence-only sex education programs, and almost everyone agrees that teenage sexual activity is not good. But if sexual promiscuity were only our modern cultural phenomenon, Solomon would not have written so much to his son about avoiding sexual sin. One-third of his "letter" to his son (the first nine chapters of

Proverbs) exhorts his son to avoid promiscuity and adultery. The surrounding culture can make sexual promiscuity easier to engage in or to avoid, but because we are sinners, sexual sin will always be enticing, especially to the young.

Sex and the Single Fool

"At the window of my house I looked out through the lattice. I saw among the simple, I noticed among the young men, a youth who lacked judgment . . ." (Prov. 7:6–7). Children are foolish. Fools don't think about consequences. They have poor judgment, lack self-control, ignore warnings, and think God isn't watching. And, as the young man of Proverbs 7 illustrates, fools fall easily into sexual sin.

Foolish teenagers are naïve about sex and reckless in their behavior. They have silly ideas about how to prevent pregnancy and are unrealistic. They think, *It'll never happen to me.*

An eighteen-year-old boy says, "I'm not going to get a girl pregnant while we're living together. We won't have sex." A young, unwed mother says, "I have this friend, she's 14. She sees me and says, 'Oh, you have a cute son. I want to be pregnant.' " This friend doesn't consider the consequences and hardships of having a baby at so young an age and outside of marriage.

Foolish teens think that sex is the most important part of a relationship. "I'm not totally against premarital sex. You need to find out if that person can satisfy you or not. Sometimes when the person doesn't satisfy you, you find out that you're not as in love as you thought," said an eighteen-year-old girl. One sixteen-year-old girl kept on hoping that sex would create love, and so "she had sex with all her crushes."

Foolish teens think they know everything and don't listen to advice. "People our age, when a grown-up talks to you, it's like they're preaching at you. You just tune it out." "She would talk to me and talk to me and talk to me. But it would go in one ear and out the other." "My parents don't know anything about sex."

They give in to the pleasures of the moment and don't weigh the consequences. "I really didn't even think about it. I didn't think it would happen to somebody like me," said a girl who became pregnant at age sixteen. Another girl who became pregnant at age fourteen said to her mother, "I don't know how to take care of a baby. I'm too scared. I'm just a little girl." They lack self-control.

They do things they regret. Eight out of ten girls who have had sex wish they had waited. Those who end up pregnant say: "There is no more childhood." "I can't do a lot of the things I used to."[3]

Most of all, foolish teens don't consider God. They look for love and fulfillment from a boyfriend or from a baby. They tell themselves that it's okay to have sex before marriage (see Prov. 30:20), they ignore their obligations to God, and they don't recognize that their "ways are in full view of the LORD" (5:21).

Because teenagers are young, foolish, and unmarried (see 1 Cor. 7:1–2, 8–9), they are particularly vulnerable to a culture that says, "Sex is fun; sex is for you." But, Solomon says, wisdom will save our daughters from sexual sin. Wisdom leads to self-control, and both wisdom and self-control develop from knowing God (Prov. 1:7; 9:10; 15:33).

Self-Control Is a Fruit of the Spirit

"Let's be realistic: teenagers are going to have sex," say teachers, physicians, and newspaper columnists. They think it is useless even to try to teach children to abstain from sex before marriage. "It's impossible. Their hormones are raging. Better teach them how to use birth control."

But the Scriptures teach that *self*-control is possible—it is a fruit of the Spirit. Sexual self-control is a particular manifestation of the spiritual fruit listed in Galatians 5:22–23.

While the world says it is inevitable that your daughter will give in to her raging hormones, the Bible says it is inevitable that your daughter will grow in self-control as she gets to know Jesus better. In a world full of sexual temptations and a culture that encourages all kinds of sexual sins, this is good news for parents.

Because God is at work in our daughters, we parents can have hope. Even though a majority of teenagers have succumbed to the sexual temptations that surround them, it doesn't mean that our daughters *will.* We can pray, expecting God to give them sexual self-control and the ability to withstand the sexual temptations they find all around them. When you ask God to nurture the fruit of self-control in your believing daughter, you are praying for what God in his Word has said he intends to do (see 1 Thess. 4:3–8). So you can pray with confidence.

Don't accept the "raging hormones" theory. Parents who expect that their teenagers will engage in sexual activity are rarely disappointed, because children live up to our expectations. If your daughter believes her biology is more powerful than her good judgment, she has no incentive to resist at the moment of temptation. But when you teach her that she has the power of the Holy Spirit to do what is right, you give *her* hope that she can control her passions, and with such hope, she is more likely to exercise self-control.

The best strategy for keeping your daughter from sexual sin is to help her know God better. When she knows God's love and goodness, she sees that his laws are for her benefit. When she understands God's holiness, she wants to be holy as he is. When she sees God's patience, she can be more patient. She expects his help because she knows he is all-powerful. She waits for him to fulfill her desires at the right time because she knows he is wise. Her self-control results from an intimate relationship with God. Pray that she would know God in such a way that she is always being conformed to the image of Jesus.

> **Application** *Teach your daughter that God produces the fruit of self-control in her when she believes in Jesus. Have her memorize Galatians 5:22–23: "But the fruit of the Spirit is love, joy, peace, patience, kindness, goodness, faithfulness, gentleness and self-control."*

Self-Control Results from Biblical Self-Understanding

"Do you not know that your body is a temple of the Holy Spirit, who is in you, whom you have received from God? You are not your own; you were bought at a price. Therefore honor God with your body," Paul wrote to the Corinthians (1 Cor. 6:19–20). Among other things, that meant that they were to "flee from sexual immorality" (v. 18). How your daughter thinks about herself affects what she does with her body. The more she knows herself from God's perspective—who she is, where she came from, and where she is going—the more she will exercise self-control.[4]

A girl who understands that she belongs to God—having been redeemed by Jesus' death for her sins, united to Christ, and given the Holy Spirit to live in her and enable her to do what is right—longs for and prays for self-control. She wants to honor God with her body (v. 20). Instead of being mastered by her sexual desires, she asks God to help her be master of her own body (vv. 12–13; 9:27; see also Phil. 3:14) so that she can pursue his holy calling. A girl who knows she belongs to God by creation and redemption wants to obey him and save sexual intercourse for marriage. She makes wise choices that keep her from sexual sins.

Common to girls who are less likely to engage in early sexual activity are loving supervision, feelings of competence, higher goals, and contentment with their own bodies. A girl who has biblical self-understanding realizes that she has all these benefits, and more, through Christ.

Self-Control Is a Lifelong Habit

Parents begin worrying about their daughters and sex just about the time their daughters start showing interest in boys. We think, *If only we can get them through the teen years and safely married!* But the ability to control her passions begins before your daughter even thinks about dating, and she will need sexual self-control even after she marries (see Prov. 5:15–20; 7:10–20).

Sexual self-control needs a foundation of other habits of self-control, such as the ability to control her emotions as a toddler. When you don't indulge her temper tantrums during the terrible twos, you are preparing your daughter to exercise self-control in sexual conduct years later. What she watches, reads, and does, the friends she chooses, the places she goes, and what she thinks about will influence whether she resists or gives in when sexual temptations present themselves now and years from now.

Talk to your daughter about making wise choices in her activities and friends. Through your own discipline, help her learn self-discipline. Be careful what television shows and movies she watches, what books and magazines she reads, and what friends she hangs out with. Teach her the consequences of sin, keep an eye on the habits she is developing, and encourage her relationship with God.

The Importance of Parents

"Surprise: Your teens want to hear from you."[5] Research, experts, parents, and teens agree: teenagers still trust their parents more than they do their peers, and teenagers who stay close to their parents are less likely to become sexually active at an early age. Parents have opportunities to teach and influence their daughters that no one else has. You are one of the most effective tools God uses to develop the fruit of self-control in your daughter.

Stay close. Girls who have a close relationship with their parents are least likely to engage in premarital sex. Hug her. Tell her you love her. Take an interest in what interests her. Girls who live with both mother and father are, as a group, the least likely to have had sex in their teen years and to have become teenage mothers. Girls especially need their fathers' affection.

The effectiveness of any list of "how to's" depends on whether your daughter knows with certainty that you love her. She needs a relationship with you that is "warm in tone, firm in discipline, and rich in communication."[6]

Application *Remember: You can't hug your daughter too often!*

Teach Biblical Values

The Scriptures have a very clear message about sexual sin—avoid it. God isn't neutral on sexual matters, and you shouldn't be either. "As long as you use birth control" isn't the Christian parent's response to teenage sexual activity. Teach your daughter that the seventh commandment means that sex is for marriage only.

As Solomon did in the book of Proverbs, warn her about the dangers and consequences of sexual sin. Premarital sex is not just "likely" to have harmful psychological and physical effects. It *will* do harm, because it goes against God's law. Let her know that the only "safe sex" is within marriage.

Talk, Talk, Talk

Talk to your daughter about love, marriage, and sex; about her future and her goals; about the Scriptures and her peers; about right and wrong; about making wise decisions; about herself and how she relates to God.

Take the time to listen to her. Share in her dreams for the future. Listen to her problems with her peer group. Answer her questions about sex honestly and as fully as is appropriate for her age. She really wants to get her information from you, so be approachable.

> **Application** *Give your daughter some Christian materials on abstinence to read, and then talk with her about it. I recommend Elisabeth Elliot, "Sex Is a Lot More Than Fun," © 1986, available through GATEWAY TO JOY, Box 82500, Lincoln, NE 68501 (1-800-759-4569) or Box 10, Winnepeg, MB R3C 2G2 (1-800-663-2425).*

Supervise and Monitor

Remember that your daughter is foolish. She needs your advice and guidance. She needs rules, curfews, and chaperones. Get to know her friends and their families. Know where she is and with whom, and as much as possible, what they are up to.

Especially supervise her dating. The earlier a girl begins to date and the bigger the age difference between her and her date, the more likely she is to engage in sexual behaviors. Encourage chaperoned group activities. Discourage one-on-one dating at a young age.

Help Her Plan for the Future

Children who have nothing else to do are drawn into trouble. Doing poorly in school is often an early warning that teen pregnancy will soon follow. But girls who are working toward the future are more likely to delay sex and pregnancy.[7]

Help your daughter learn to do something well; keep her busy; praise her successes. Help her set long-term goals and plan the steps to reach them. Remind her that her purpose in life is to glorify God, build his kingdom on earth, and enjoy him forever.

Teach Her Strategies to Resist Temptation

One out of three girls who have had sex did not plan on it the first time. Eighty percent of teenage girls who have had sex wish they had waited.[8] Before she ever leaves your front door with a boy, teach your daughter precautions that can help keep her from becoming sexually active.

Teach her "the law of diminishing returns" in sexual thrills.[9] At first holding hands is exciting, but soon she gets used to that sensation and the excitement wears off. Now she starts kissing, but soon that isn't exciting enough either. So she goes on to the next level, and the next, until she arrives at full contact sex. Urge your daughter not to put the law of diminishing returns into motion. Teach her to delay touching.

Teach her the art of conversation. "Young lovebirds usually choose between talking and touching. They don't do both simultaneously. My preference is for my daughter to talk!" wrote one father about the importance of learning to talk to each other.[10] Teach her to communicate clearly her beliefs and expectations. Explain that by talking instead of touching, she will really get to know the young man and whether he is or isn't the kind of man God wants for her.

Teach her how to make wise decisions, avoid bad situations, and stand up for what she believes in the face of peer pressure. Train her to ask herself, *How will I feel tomorrow if I do this now?* Warn her about situations that make sexual sin harder to resist. Remind her to apply God's Word even in the little decisions she makes.

Make sure she knows that you will always come and get her, no matter where she is or what time it is. Tell her that you will always support her decision to back out of any situation that makes her uncomfortable or afraid.

Teach her to pray and hide God's Word in her heart. Explain that God never puts her in a place where she must sin. Remind her that God always provides a way out of temptation and that the Holy Spirit gives her the strength not to sin.

Application *Whenever your daughter leaves your house—whether it is a date, a sleepover, or a party—make sure that she has the ability to call you. Give her a cellular phone, "mad money," or a prepaid phone card. Remind her that you're just a phone call away if she needs you.*

Enlist Other Adults

You are the most important and influential adult in your daughter's life, but you don't have to go it alone. Build a network of adults who reinforce the values that lead to sexual self-control. Look for adults who are good role models and who will encourage your daughter to plan for a good future, stand up for what she believes in, and love and obey God. Look for activities, clubs, or groups that can help her develop responsibility, a feeling of competence, and a close relationship with another adult. Foster close relationships with her grandparents, aunts and uncles, and the parents of her friends. Take her to church and Sunday school.

Find a group of parents who share your values. Talk to other parents in your church, in your neighborhood, and at school. Get to know the parents of your daughter's friends (and especially any boyfriends). Make sure you are in agreement with them about chaperones, parties, dating, curfews, and what is acceptable behavior for teens and what isn't.

Encourage Good Character

Character is what she does when you are not looking. An enterprising and determined child can get around most rules, and parents can't supervise a child twenty-four hours a day for her entire life. How she behaves in her bedroom, on dates, and in her marriage depends on what kind of character she has developed.

You teach her good character by displaying good character yourself, by discouraging her wrong behavior and nurturing her good behavior, and by pointing her toward God. Talk about the fruit of the Spirit and how we can display love, joy, peace, patience, kindness, goodness, faithfulness, humility, and self-control in our everyday lives. Talk about how true love waits, how sin destroys our peace, how God strengthens our weaknesses, and how God always gives us a way out of temptation (1 Cor. 10:13). Hold Jesus up as her standard and example (see 1 Cor. 11:1; Eph. 5:1–2).

Not the Unforgivable Sin

One day a father called and asked if his daughter could come and talk to me. "I know something is wrong, but she won't tell me what it is," he said. What was wrong was that she had committed a sexual sin, and although she had stopped the behavior and confessed to God, she felt guilty.

As David did, sometimes sincere believers commit sexual sins (see 2 Sam. 11:2–5; 1 Cor. 5:1; 2 Cor. 12:20–21). About half of young people in evangelical churches have engaged in sexual behaviors. While we all hope our daughters will not be among those who do, temptations in our modern world are strong, opportunities are plentiful, and we are all sinners. What can you do if your daughter commits sexual sin?

First, assure her that, although sexual sins carry consequences that some other sins do not (see, for example, 1 Cor. 6:18), it is *not* the unforgivable sin or even the worst sin. Assure her that God forgives sexual sins just as he does others (1 John 1:9). If your daughter is a sincere believer, her heart will be very heavy over this particular sin, and on top of that, she may be afraid of your reaction as well. Treat her with tenderness, and lead her to repentance. Remember that we all struggle with sin (Rom. 3:23; 7:21–25; 1 Cor. 10:13).

Second, assure her that by God's grace she can live a new life (see 2 Cor. 5:17; Gal. 5:16–25; Col. 3:1–17). Then help her make a plan to avoid sexual sin in the future. This may include keeping her busy, chaperoned, or away from friends and situations that make sin easier. Don't let her spend time alone with her boyfriend. Ground her if necessary. Help her save this special relationship for marriage, as God intended.

Is the Sexual Revolution Over?

After thirty years, the sexual revolution shows signs of fizzling. Statistics over the last few years show a steadily decreasing percentage of teens engaging in sexual activity. Society is reaching consensus that we do not want our teenagers to be sexually active, and teenage attitudes are changing. Ninety-five percent of teenagers say it is important to give teens a strong message on abstinence; nine out of ten say that teenagers are not prepared to have babies; and six out of ten disapprove of premarital sex.[11]

Society may be becoming friendlier to Christian values on sex, but this doesn't mean our job as parents is done. Downward trends can always turn upward again, as they have with drug use. Television shows, movies, and song lyrics have not gotten cleaner. People are still sinners, and teenagers are still foolish.

Be glad when society changes for the better—but be wise, and teach your daughter to be wise. The better your daughter knows God, the more she will want to do what he says is right, the more she will develop the fruit of the Spirit, and the less likely she will be to commit sexual sins.

For Further Thought and Discussion

1. Read Proverbs 5:1–23; 6:20–7:27; and 9:13–18. How is the adulteress like the woman Folly? Why do folly and sexual sin go together?

2. Read Proverbs 31:10–31. How is the excellent wife different from the fool and the adulteress? How would characteristics such as doing good to others (especially her husband) (v. 11), speaking with wisdom (v. 26), not being idle (v. 27), and fearing the Lord (v. 30) relate to sexual self-control?

3. Read Galatians 5:16–25. How does living by the Spirit influence our ability to resist the desires of the sinful nature? How would having love, patience, and the other fruit strengthen sexual self-control?

4. Read 2 Samuel 11:1–12:25; Psalm 51; 1 Corinthians 6:12–20; and 1 John 1:9. Should we consider sexual sin worse than lying or gluttony? How are sexual sins different from some other sins? How are sexual sins like all other sins? Are sexual sins forgivable?

Points for Prayer

❧ Pray that God would make your daughter wise in whom
she dates, where she goes, and what she does.

❧ Pray that your daughter would love God above all others.

*" 'Love the Lord your God with all your heart and with all your soul and with all
your mind.' This is the first and greatest commandment. And the second is like it:
'Love your neighbor as yourself.' " —Matthew 22:37–39*

CHAPTER 15

Teach Her to Be Wise in Dating

The young men Zeke's daughters dated invariably turned out to be shy and reserved. Not one tried to hold a hand or steal a good-night kiss—because, before any date left with one of his daughters, Zeke had invited the young man down to see his model trains, where he delivered this basement lecture:

> Listen, kid, I was a young guy once myself. And I know what young guys think about when it comes to girls. I know that you've got one thing on your mind.
>
> So let me tell you what I'll do if you try any funny stuff with my daughter. I'll hurt you real bad. I mean, you'll feel terrible pain. . . .

And since Zeke was an ex-paratrooper and built like an NFL lineman, the young men believed him. Zeke said, "I raised very good girls. And I helped their dates be very good boys."[1] Zeke would be welcome in the Secret Council of Fathers of Daughters any day.

Dating was not part of the culture when the Old and New Testaments were written. In those days, marriages were arranged, and in some countries they still are. The closer our daughters got to the age at which boyfriends are old enough to have driver's licenses, the less we liked the idea of dating. Does that mean John and I are planning to arrange our daughters' marriages to eligible young men of our acquaintance? No, but we are looking to the Scriptures for wisdom in our cultural situation.

The Bible gives us guidelines that answer the questions Whom should I date? Where should we go? What should we do? The Bible tells us to avoid bad companions (1 Cor. 15:33; Prov. 13:20) and situations that make it easier to sin (Ps. 1:1–2; Prov. 1:15–16; 7:6–9), to do good to our neighbor (Ps. 15:1–3; Prov. 14:21) and not cause another to stumble into sin (1 Cor. 10:31–33), to avoid sexual immorality (1 Thess. 4:3–7), and to love God above all others (Deut. 5:7). If you apply these guidelines and teach them to your daughter, you will be acting wisely and teaching her to do the same.

Remember the Law of Diminishing Returns

One day your daughter mentions a boy in her class and says he's really cool. Soon a boy is on the phone asking to speak to your daughter. A few months later she asks you to drive her and a girl friend to a movie so that they can meet two boys. Then comes the day when a young man pulls up in the driveway and announces that he is there to pick up your daughter.

As your daughter grows up, she becomes interested in boys and they become interested in her. But the earlier she starts dating, the sooner she starts holding hands and kissing, and the more she and her date are alone, the more likely she is to engage in sexual activity. As we noted in the previous chapter, this is "the law of diminishing returns." You and your daughter can counteract this tendency by giving it less time and opportunity to work.

What Parents Can Do

Delay Dating. The younger a girl begins dating, the more likely she is to engage in sexual activity. It is also more likely that she will have multiple sexual partners during her teenage years. She is less likely to use birth control and more likely to become pregnant. She is at greater risk for venereal diseases and even cervical cancer.

For your daughter's well-being, delay the dating process. Let her social contacts with boys take place within group settings such as an after-school club or church youth group day hike. Keep her boyfriends at the friendship level until you think she has the maturity to handle real dating. Ellie's first "boyfriends" talked with her on the phone a lot, rarely saw her, and still needed parents to drive them to the movies or the football game. She had the experience of getting to know a boy without the risks of actually being alone with him. A friendship maintained at a safe distance can still be a real and valuable relationship.

Chaperone. Group activities are a way to delay dating, but not all group activities are equally good. The summer before ninth grade, Cayenne went to a party with ten boys, ten girls, no parents, and plenty of alcohol. Within the first hour, she had had sexual intercourse for the first time.[2] When I mentioned this story to Ellie, she said, "Oh, make-out parties. Kids in my class have those."

Where are the parents? You cannot assume they are at the party your daughter has been invited to attend. Before you let your daughter accept an invitation, know the parents who are hosting the party. Make sure they will actually be there and supervising.

When your daughter begins dating, encourage her and her friend to participate in group activities, and limit the amount of time they are alone. Remember that "dating"—sending two young people out for hours alone together—is a modern phenomenon. They can still get to know each other with other people around.

Enforce Curfews. The later your daughter is out, the more likely it is that she and her date are no longer at the movies or the basketball game, the more likely they are to be alone, and the more likely they are to run out of things to say to each other. They will be more tired and sleepy and likely to cuddle. The later your daughter is out with nothing much to do or say, the more likely she is to engage in sexual activity. Protect your daughter by setting and enforcing a curfew.

What Your Daughter Can Do

Rules and supervision have only a limited effectiveness. If your daughter is determined to break your rules and God's laws, she will certainly find a time and place to do it. She must develop the good character necessary to make wise choices when you are not around. She herself must give the law of diminishing returns less to work with.

Talk, Don't Touch. We saw in the previous chapter that the law of diminishing returns operates on physical contact, whereas conversation provides a fuller knowledge of the other person.

Even though Mark and Shannon were engaged, they were usually on opposite sides of a room. They never sat next to each other on the sofa, and we never saw them hold hands. Their first kiss was after the minister said, "I now pronounce you husband and wife." Yet they knew each other very well. They had served on a summer mission together in Uganda. They had talked about their interests and goals and what each wanted to do in the future. Each had gotten to know the other's family. They knew how many children each wanted, how soon, and how they would raise them. Each knew the depth of the other's commitment to God. They went to church together, prayed together, and helped each other in a ministry to college students.

Unlike the foolish teen who believed that sex would tell her if she was in love, Mark and Shannon knew that the thrill of touching would hide their true relationship and give them the wrong foundation for marriage. Many an unhappy person has married because "the sex was great," only to discover later that the relationship wasn't.

The best way to get to know another person is by talking to him and by being around him in different situations. How does he treat others and interact with his parents? How does he study or work? How well does he accept responsibility? What activities are important to him? These are not the things a young woman can find out through a sexual relationship.

Avoid Situations That Make It Easier to Sin. Proverbs 7 describes a foolish young man seduced by a persuasive woman (v. 21). Though he follows her "all at once" (v. 22), his down-fall begins earlier when he allows himself to be in the right place at the right time to be seduced (vv. 6–20).

Most girls don't plan to have sex on a particular date. In fact, three out of four girls say they have sex because of their boyfriends' initiative.[3] One thing leads to another, passions are high, the boy says, "If you loved me you would" or "What are you afraid of; it'll be great," and in the heat of the moment, like the young fool, she is persuaded.

Elisabeth Elliot's advice to young people is succinct: "Keep hands off, clothes on, and stay out of bed."[4] This is not a com-plete list, but it is certainly easy to remember, and it makes a good test question: What decisions must she make to keep hands off, clothes on, and stay out of bed? Will being alone in the car, parked under a starry sky and a full moon, help her keep hands off and clothes on, or will it make sin easier? Will being together in an empty house make it easier to end up in bed? Teach your daughter to evaluate her actions and activities by whether or not they will help her keep hands off, clothes on, and stay out of bed.

Show True Love. "True love conquers all," the wicked fairy tells the Prince in Disney's *Cinderella*. "How can I tell if this is true love?" young people ask. "True love waits," adults reply.

True love does overcome obstacles and true love is patient, but "true love" does not have to be romantic love. True love fulfills God's law by doing good and not harm to a neighbor (Lev. 19:18; Ps. 15:1–3; Matt. 22:34–40; Rom. 13:8–10).

God commands our daughters to have this kind of love for everyone; even an enemy is a neighbor (Matt. 5:43–48; Luke 10:25–37). Certainly boys in general, and dates especially, fall under the category of neighbors to whom your daughter should do good and not harm. It doesn't matter whether that boy or this date is her "one true love." The question your daughter should ask is not so much How can I find true love? as How can *I show* true love that fulfills God's law and helps others come to Christ?

A girl who has learned to show true love will not do things that might cause another person to stumble into sin (1 Cor. 10:32–33). She will not try to be sexually provocative by the way she dresses or acts. She will not have sex before marriage—even if her steady boyfriend asks her to—because she knows that sexual sin is not in his or her own spiritual best interests (Gal. 5:13–14). She thinks about how her actions will affect the other person's relationship with God (see 1 Cor. 10:33).

Teach your daughter what true love is. When her boyfriend says, "If you loved me you would . . ." she will have an even better answer than, "If you loved me, you wouldn't ask." She can say, "True love is doing what is best for the other person. I want to do what is best for you. God says sex is for marriage only, so I am not going to help you sin. I want you to know God better." If the boy argues, "You just don't love me enough!" she can reply, "I love you too much!"

Application *Teach your daughter that true love fulfills God's law and helps others come to Christ. Have her memorize Romans 13:10: "Love does no harm to its neighbor. Therefore love is the fulfillment of the law"; and 1 Corinthians 10:32–33: "Do not cause anyone to stumble. . . . For I am not seeking my own good but the good of many, so that they may be saved."*

Urge Her to Choose Her Boyfriends Wisely

Marie had spectacularly bad taste in boyfriends. One boy was emotionally unstable, was placed in a foster home because of severe disciplinary problems, and was constantly in trouble at school. She broke up with him and started dating a man who was eight years older than she, already had fathered one child out of wedlock, and was arrested for stealing cars. Marie always picked boys in trouble. She thought if she loved them, they would turn into responsible young men. They never did.

Marie's parents felt that anything bad they said about her boyfriends would only make her more determined and that before long she would wake up and realize what losers they were. So they never interfered. But by age sixteen, Marie was pregnant.

After numerous and even violent fights with her family, Marie moved in with the father of her child. She just barely finished high school. The couple made plans to marry, but he never seemed to have the money to buy a marriage license, and a year later Marie moved back in with her parents. They breathed a sigh of relief and thought finally she had learned something. But before long she had a new boyfriend, and one day, without a word to anyone, Marie abandoned her young daughter and moved with him to another state. Her life continues to unfold like a soap opera.

The boyfriends your daughter chooses will have enormous influence on how her life turns out. The boys she dates will influence what friends she keeps, whether she smokes or takes drugs, what she does on a Friday evening, and even how well she does in school.

Marie chose boys of poor character and, at fifteen, she dated a man in his twenties. She made poor choices, and her parents didn't correct them. You can avoid making the same mistake by helping your daughter learn to make wise choices about the age and character of her dates.

Age Differences

One day a friend asked Ellie to go to a drive-in movie. "Who else is going?" we asked. It turned out that this was a double date, and the other "boy" was twenty-one years old. We said no. "It's not that we don't trust you," John said. "We don't trust *him*."

There is good reason not to trust twenty-one-year-old men around thirteen-year-old girls. The greater the age difference between a teenage girl and her date, the more at risk she is of being seduced or even raped, of becoming sexually active at a younger age, of becoming pregnant, and of going on to have multiple sexual partners during her teenage years.[5]

The younger your daughter is, the more age differences matter, because the greater their "power imbalance."[6] A twenty-five year old is more on par with a twenty-nine year old than a fifteen year old is with a nineteen year old. The younger your daughter is, the more "growing up" she has to do, the less experience she has, and the less sure she is of herself. If her date is much older than she is, they have different experiences and expectations. She is still living at home and dependent on her parents; he may be on his own in college or working. She may be afraid to contradict him or say no; he may use persuasions she hasn't heard before and has no idea how to refuse. She may go along with what he asks, even if it seems wrong or makes her uncomfortable.

Be careful about age differences, but remember: More important than his age is what *kind* of young man he is.

Character

Foolish girls find the "bad boy" romantically attractive. Like Marie, some want to change him with their true love; they want to rescue him. Others think their "rebel without a cause" is just plain exciting; they like life in the fast lane. Foolish girls don't consider the real-life consequences of their boyfriends' habits of heavy drinking, lavish spending, or fits of temper. Foolish girls don't stop to consider character when their hearts are aflutter.

Encourage your daughter to stop and ask, *What kind of character does this boy show by what he does?* Girls who have learned to be wise know that good character is more important than good looks or a flashy car or popularity or the ability to sink a basket from beyond the three-point line. We want our daughters to look for young men who love God, who want to live by God's Word, who show a growing understanding of God and his Word, and who teach others to love God. The most important questions your daughter can ask about any young man are What is his relationship to God? and How does he show that relationship by what he does?

Application Ask questions about any boy your daughter likes. Teach her to find out the important things about him: what his relationship is to God, and how he shows that relationship by what he does. Help her evaluate a boy's character and see how that affects the way he will treat her and others, how he will carry out his responsibilities, how reliable he is, what he will be like in ten years, and so forth.

Teach Her to Love God Above All Others

"I don't feel good about myself unless a guy likes me. I do whatever it takes," said fourteen-year-old Rosemary. Seventeen-year-old Lizzie consented to have sex with her boyfriend even though she herself didn't really want to become sexually active at that time. Fourteen-year-old Holly attempted suicide after her boyfriend broke up with her. "My life is over," she said.[7] Each of these girls put a boyfriend in the place only God should have.

Girls can get so wrapped up in having a boyfriend that it becomes the most important thing to them. They want the popularity or the feeling that someone really loves them. They think they need a boyfriend to be happy or feel worthwhile. They remain stubbornly loyal to a boyfriend whom they see as a loser and whom they really don't even like that much. They are more eager to please a boyfriend than to follow their own consciences, obey their parents, or keep God's commands.

Your daughter wants companionship—God made her this way (Gen. 2:18–25). But she must seek this companionship in a way that puts God above all others (Deut. 5:7). Teach her that putting God first means being content whether or not she has a boyfriend (see 1 Cor. 7:17; Phil. 4:11–13). It means trusting that God gives her all she needs and at just the right time (see Matt. 6:25–34).

For Further Thought and Discussion

1. Read Deuteronomy 5:7; Proverbs 7:6–9; 13:20; 14:21; 1 Corinthians 10:31–33; and 1 Thessalonians 4:3–7. How do these verses answer the questions "What should I do when my daughter wants to date?" "Whom should my daughter date?" "What should she do on a date?" What other guidelines does Scripture give parents and children that apply to dating?

2. Read Proverbs 7. How does the young fool end up in the right place at the right time to be seduced? How could he have avoided this sin?

3. Read Matthew 22:34–40; Romans 13:8–10; Galatians 5:13–25; and 1 Corinthians 13:4–8a. How does true love fulfill God's law? How is true love different from the popular view of romantic love? How should true love affect sexual conduct? How should true love fit in with romantic love?

4. Read Deuteronomy 5:7; 6:5; Matthew 6:33; and Philippians 4:11–13. How does putting God first make us content with our circumstances? How does putting God first affect what we do?

Points for Prayer

❧ Pray that God would lead your daughter to a man of good character.

❧ Pray that God would make your daughter a woman of good character.

" 'For this reason a man will leave his father and mother and be united to his wife, and the two will become one flesh.' This a profound mystery. . . ." —Ephesians 5:31–32a

CHAPTER 16

Teach Her God's Way of Marriage

"Don't you believe in marriage?" a character in the comic strip Beetle Bailey asks Miss Buxley. The young secretary replies, "I don't *need* to get married, I'm a whole person. Even if the right guy comes along, we don't have to get *married*. Even if I *get* married, I don't have to *believe* in it . . . even if I *believe* in it, I don't . . ."[1]

Fewer and fewer people today seem to believe in marriage. Divorce is up, as is the number of people who have never married, the number of cohabiting couples, and the number of unmarried couples with children. Smith College offered only the following choices on its twenty-fifth reunion fact sheet: "single," "divorced," "widowed," "living with someone."[2] These days it's hard to know whether the omission of "married" on the form was a mistake or an assumption!

Though people have romantic ideas about love and high expectations of a mate,[3] they are confused about what marriage is and ambivalent about whether it's important. They want someone to love, and they want to be loved. But they don't want to make a commitment, they don't want to lose their independence, and they are afraid to trust anyone. They plan their lives expecting divorce.

Many teenagers have become cynical about marriage. They prefer living together without marriage because they have seen their parents divorce or they listen to their parents' constant arguing. Their high school and college textbooks are "determinedly pessimistic" about marriage.[4] Feminists tell girls that marriage is actually bad for women.

One of the best things you can do for your daughter is have a good marriage—and not only because of the social advantages, but because you give her an example. She sees how a man and a woman show love to one another. She sees how husband and wife help each other, support each other, listen to each other, work out problems, resolve conflicts, and have fun together. She sees how God makes two people one.

Application *If you are a single parent, look for couples who have strong and loving marriages that can serve as examples to your daughter.*

Created for Marriage

As God created the sky, earth, and seas, the sun and the moon, plants and animals, he pronounced them "good." The only thing he didn't find good was that Adam was alone, and so God made a helper suitable for Adam—a woman (Gen. 2:18–24). God made man and woman to enjoy the closeness of marriage as they fulfill their purpose of glorifying and enjoying God and building his kingdom.

Your daughter longs for love because she was made to, and finding love *is* a good thing (see Prov. 18:22). But society says—through its songs, movies, and example—that she doesn't need marriage to have the kind of love that God created a man and a woman to share.

Parents used to assume their daughters would marry and have a family, but daughters who marry and then have children have become a minority.[5] As the social rules relax, it is even more important than it was a generation ago to teach your daughter God's way of marriage.

Marriage Is a Good Thing

"He who finds a wife finds a good thing" (Prov. 18:22 NASB). Marriage is good because God made it for expressing love, for help and companionship, and for rearing children (Gen. 1:27–31; 3:18–25). Marriage is the basic building block of a good society. There is no substitute. Only in marriage will your daughter find the commitment and structure for love, sex, and children.

Living together without marriage is not "a good thing." It breaks God's command and leads to a list of social ills. You can open your daughter's eyes to the liabilities of living together without marriage.

- Couples who live together and then marry have higher divorce rates.
- A live-in girlfriend doesn't have the legal status and protections of a wife.
- A father is more likely to leave his children when there is no legal marriage.
- Children are more likely to be abused when the mother lives with a man who is not her husband.

Married people live longer and happier lives, and so do their children. Marriage is a blessing and a gift from God.

Marriage Is Oneness

In God's mathematics, one man plus one woman equals one in marriage (Gen. 2:24). Marriage reflects the "profound mystery" of Christ and the church (Eph. 5:22–33). It pictures the love, fellowship, and intimacy of the relationship between God the Father and Jesus (see 1 Cor. 11:3) and between Jesus and believers (see Rev. 19:6–9).

Marriage is more than a "piece of paper" that creates legal

roadblocks for two people who might want to go their separate ways. It is two people becoming one. They work toward the same goals. They share their money and their material possessions. They trust one another. They make sacrifices out of love for each other (see 1 Cor. 13:4–8a). Even their own bodies belong each one to the other (1 Cor. 7:3–4). The best interests of one *are* the best interests of the other.

Because marriage is oneness, a bride is not taking on a permanent roommate or a convenient sex partner. She is becoming one with her husband in finances and material goods, in goals and dreams, in heart, mind, and body.

Application *Find out what your daughter thinks marriage is. What does she expect out of marriage, from a husband, in childrearing, with finances, about sex, and so forth?*

Marriage Is a Covenant

Our premarital counseling was short but to the point. The minister who was to marry us had baptized me, and so he knew me well; but he was meeting John for the first time. He leaned over, looked John in the eye, and said, "Son, I hope you don't consider divorce an option, because I don't marry couples who consider divorce an option."

Teach your daughter that marriage is a covenant, a promise made to her husband before God to remain faithful to each other until one of the two dies. It is a promise to work at this relationship, to resolve conflicts, to stick together through good times and through bad, when it is easy to feel love and when it is hard.

Because marriage is a commitment to become one in heart, mind, and body and to stick together through easy times and hard times, which man your daughter marries is one of the most important decisions she will make. Marriage with a bad husband is full of grief (see Prov. 12:4; 19:13; 21:9), but when she chooses the right person, marriage is a very good thing.

Application *Read 1 Corinthians 13 in family devotions and talk about each characteristic of love. Have her memorize 1 Corinthians 13:4–8a: "Love is patient, love is kind. It does not envy, it does not boast, it is not proud. It is not rude, it is not self-seeking, it is not easily angered, it keeps no record of wrongs. Love does not delight in evil but rejoices with the truth. It always protects, always trusts, always hopes, always perseveres. Love never fails."*

Choose the Right Man

A teenager's idea of love is formed more by the latest hit movie than by real life. She thinks *Romeo and Juliet* is so romantic. She thinks the bad boy who mistreats her will turn into her hero. She thinks lasting love comes at first sight. She has her head in the clouds, and she needs you to help her keep her feet on the ground.

Pastors, therapists, and divorce lawyers complain that by the time they see couples in their offices, they have already made their choices. Few engaged couples will break up when marriage is only months away. Few couples filing for divorce are willing to reconcile. Most couples don't seek advice early enough. As a parent, you have opportunities years before your daughter is even dating to teach her to make a wise choice.

Your daughter is going to marry a sinner. As Elisabeth Elliot says, "There's nobody else to marry."[6] No matter which man she marries, she will have to overlook imperfections and forgive faults (see 1 Cor. 13:4–7; 1 Peter 4:8). But some habits and characteristics should be warning signs. Your daughter should be careful *which sinner* she marries.

The important question is whether he is a *forgiven* sinner, a man who knows and wants to please Jesus. He won't be perfect, but does she see evidence that the fruit of the Spirit is growing in him? Does he try to apply the Word in the way he lives and the decisions he makes? A man who knows God will show habits of godliness. Does he?

Habits of godliness are the first characteristics she should look for, but there are other questions she should ask and answer.

Can We Talk?

"How well do you communicate? Are you having any trouble?" pastors and other counselors ask engaged couples in pre-marital sessions. "Everything is great," they always reply; "we're in love." Yet the typical complaints of married couples are that they don't communicate and they don't resolve conflicts.[7]

In marriage, there will be conflict, hurt feelings, misunderstandings, differences of opinion, honest mistakes, and deliberate injuries. Good communication between husband and wife will help them have fewer misunderstandings and talk through the conflicts. She and he must be able to talk honestly and freely about anything and everything. She should be able to tell him more than she would even tell her best girl friend.

Do I Want to Follow Him?

Comedians and comic strip creators make jokes of the contempt many married couples feel for each other. But God's way of marriage is the opposite: a husband loves his wife as he loves himself and treats her with respect, and a wife loves and respects her husband and defers to his lead (Eph. 5:21–33; 1 Peter 3:1–8; see also Prov. 31:11–12, 28). God has given the husband the position of leadership in marriage (see 1 Cor. 11:3; Eph. 5:23). That statement gets the feminists out with their protest signs, because headship and submission in marriage have been misunderstood, maligned, and misused. The Scriptures teach that husband and wife are equals (see Gen. 1:27; Gal. 3:26–28) who have different responsibilities in marriage (Eph. 5:22–33).[8]

The husband should use his authority in the best interests of his wife and win her trust and devotion through his gentleness and self-sacrifice. He shouldn't hold his position with a heavy hand. He should recognize her value, confide in her, listen to her opinions, and ask her advice (see Prov. 31:10–29). The wife should recognize her husband's God-given dignity as head of the family. She should respect his abilities, trust his decisions, have high regard for his opinions, and be confident in his motives. Each should respect the other; each should serve the other; each should want the best for the other.

Your daughter must ask, *Do I respect him, and does he respect me?* Does she value his abilities, trust his judgment, and find his opinions persuasive? Do they agree most of the time? Can they have a difference of opinion, discuss it, and still like each other? Is he overbearing, or gentle? Whose interests does he usually put first, hers or his own? Is his love self-centered or self-sacrificing? Can she see herself gladly agreeing to follow *him?*

Do I Want Him to Be the Father of My Children?

Would your daughter be happy to see her own children grow up to act as he does? Does he have the habits she would want to see in her own children? Is he respectful to his parents, patient with other people's children, gentle and considerate with her? Does he even want children? How would he discipline them? Is he responsible, or selfish? Does he show the character that makes a good father?

Do I Want to Grow Old with Him?

It is contrary to the foolish nature of the young to think about growing old or becoming disabled. They don't expect good looks to fade, health to fail, or strength to turn feeble. They may not focus on the person underneath that attractive exterior. How would she feel if *her* Superman became a quadriplegic?

Teach your daughter to look beyond the attraction of youth and beauty and ask, *Do I want to grow old with him?* Is the person underneath attractive enough still to excite her when she and he are sixty-four (see Prov. 5:15–19; Mal. 2:13–15)? Does he expect her to get a face-lift at thirty-nine? Does she expect him not to lose his hair? Is the main attraction between them good looks and athletic ability, or character and personality?

Finding the right person is only half of the happily-ever-after equation, however. To be happy in marriage, your daughter must also learn to be the right woman.

Be the Right Woman

More and more people are marrying two, three, even four or more times. "Encore marriages" run a greater risk of divorce than do first marriages because people take the same character and habits from one marriage into the next, and the next. "The wise woman builds her house, but with *her own hands* the foolish one tears hers down" (Prov. 14:1).

A quick temper, lying, jealousy, poor judgment, pride, selfishness, and self-indulgence have ruined many marriages. Fools are self-destructive; sin has natural consequences; "misfortune pursues the sinner" (13:21). But the Lord "blesses the home of the righteous" (3:33). A woman who has learned to please God builds a happy marriage by her behavior (see 16:7). She turns away anger by a gentle answer (15:1), speaks honestly (24:26), doesn't let disputes grow (10:12; 12:16; 17:14), works diligently (10:4–5; 13:4), and gives generously (11:24–26).

Proverbs 31:10–31 describes the wife of good character. She is generous, patient, loving, and wise. She does good to those around her (see also 12:4). She controls her tongue. She is not lazy (see also 1 Tim. 5:13; Titus 2:3–5). She has inner beauty because she fears the Lord. She has "all the virtues and strengths of character urged upon us throughout Proverbs."9 She is both able *and* willing to help her husband.

Able to Help

Just reading the exploits of the noble wife of Proverbs 31 makes real women tired. She gets up before dawn and burns the midnight oil. She deals in real estate and trades on the stock market. She owns a clothing factory and runs a vineyard. She is an interior designer and a fashion consultant. She teaches and does community volunteer work. She spins her own thread, weaves her own cloth, sews all her children's clothes, cooks four-star meals—and still has time and energy for her husband!

Fortunately for real women, the noble wife is a composite picture. She represents, not one SuperWife, but the possibilities. One woman may do some of these things with greater or lesser skill, but women *can* do all these things. Women can own businesses, excel in the creative arts, be inspiring teachers, have gifts for helping others, and manage a household.

A helper who has no skills is not very useful. God has given your daughter talents. Help her develop them. Encourage her to study hard, learn a wide variety of skills, and excel where God has given her ability. Tell her that the right man will appreciate (and need) her talents.

Willing to Help

Your daughter probably hears a lot about "girl power," but self-sacrifice is a forgotten virtue. It is our nature to be selfish. No wonder feminists emphasize competence and equality and disdain submission and service.

In God's kingdom, however, the servant is the greatest of all; submission and service make us most like Jesus, who came to serve (Matt. 20:28) and do his Father's will (John 6:38). He "did not consider equality with God something to be grasped, but made himself nothing, taking the very nature of a servant" (Phil. 2:6–7) in order to save his people (John 6:38–40; Heb. 10:5–10).

Your daughter needs not only the skills to help but also the attitude that characterized Jesus (Phil. 2:3–8). A helper who is not willing to help is a contradiction.

The noble wife of Proverbs 31 is a willing helper. She is compassionate and generous (vv. 15, 20). She works hard for the benefit of others (vv. 11–12, 15, 21). She brings honor to her husband (v. 23) and doesn't brag about herself (vv. 26, 28–31). She knows that those who push themselves forward for notice and honor never get it (see 25:6–7, 27; Matt. 23:5–12; Luke 14:7–11).

Help your daughter to see that love gives; love isn't selfish or jealous. When she loves her husband, she will want to pro-mote his happiness, look out for his best interests, and help him accomplish his goals. She will be his equal, but out of love for him and obedience to God (Eph. 5:22–24), she must be willing to submit and serve in order to build God's kingdom. Teach your daughter that through submission and service in marriage she imitates Jesus and shows the world what he is like.

Application *Read Ephesians 5:21–33 in family devotions. Talk about the duties of husband and wife. Ask, How does Christ show his love for the church? Why would a wife submit to her husband? What does it mean to submit "as to the Lord"? To love another as one's own body? Talk about how both husband and wife imitate Christ by loving and serving each other.*

A Woman of Noble Character

The best way to ensure that your daughter has a happy marriage is to encourage her good character now. When you teach her to be patient, to love her brother or sister, to respect her grandparents, to tell the truth, or to give to the needy, you are helping her develop the character she needs to be happy in marriage. Without wisdom, kindness, faithfulness, humility, and self-control, she is unlikely to have a successful marriage.

These qualities come from God. If you want your daughter to be happy in marriage, teach her to love God with all her heart, mind, body, and soul. The wife of good character is happy in marriage because she knows, loves, and obeys God.

Application *Read Proverbs 31:10–31 in family devotions. Talk about the qualities of the wife of noble character. Ask, Is the wife of noble character different from what you hear a woman should be like? Why does her husband have full confidence in her? Why does she look forward to the future? Why isn't she afraid of growing old? Why do so many people like her? What does she need to know and do to be this kind of woman?*

For Further Thought and Discussion

1. Why do you think so many people today don't "believe" in marriage? Is your daughter at risk of developing a cynical attitude toward marriage? How can you help her view marriage as a good thing?

2. Read Genesis 1:27–31; 2:18–25; Proverbs 18:22; and Ephesians 5:22–33. Why did God make marriage? In what ways is marriage good?

3. Read Malachi 2:11–16; Matthew 5:31–32; 19:3–10; and 1 Corinthians 7:10–17. Why does God hate divorce? Why does God permit divorce? In what circumstances? Why did the disciples think it would be better not to marry? If divorces were harder to obtain today, do you think people would be more cautious about getting married, would enter marriage with greater commitment, and/or would work harder to reconcile in marriage? Why or why not?

4. Read 1 Corinthians 13:4–8a. List the characteristics of love. How would such love help a couple keep their covenant of marriage?

5. Read Proverbs 31:10–31; Matthew 20:20–28; Ephesians 5:21–33; and 1 Peter 3:1–8. What is a wife's duty to her husband? What is a husband's duty to his wife? How does the world view authority and submission? How would you describe submission and headship in marriage from these passages? How should mutual love and respect color the relationship between husband and wife?

6. Read Proverbs 14:1; 24:3–4; and 31:10–31. List the qualities of a wife of noble character. How do these characteristics "build her house"? How would the lack of them tear it down? What "rare and beautiful treasures" do you want in your home? In your daughter's home?

Points for Prayer

🦋 Pray that God would so unite your daughter to Jesus that she would be like him in her actions and her attitudes.

🦋 Pray that your daughter would understand the characteristics of sin and the character of God.

"A woman of noble character . . . is worth far more than rubies. . . . Charm is deceptive, and beauty is fleeting; but a woman who fears the LORD is to be praised." —Proverbs 31:10, 30

CHAPTER 17

A Daughter of Good Character

At age twenty, Stacy broke her neck in a diving accident and was paralyzed from the neck down. The doctors told her parents that she would never walk again, but she did regain use of her hands and now walks with crutches. Her legs are always cold, she rarely sleeps through the night, and she depends on other people to help with her laundry or to vacuum her room. But she doesn't let her circumstances determine her state of mind. She works in a ministry to college students because she knows that joy and strength are found in a relationship with Jesus Christ.[1]

Nineteen-year-old Elizabeth was serving as a short-term missionary in China when she needed emergency surgery. During her week of recovery, she was patient and used her "unusual vacation" as an opportunity to learn more about God. Even though her plans were disrupted, she knew that God's plans were better than hers and that he did not need her to accomplish his work. Rather than complaining, she thanked God.[2]

In the middle of the night, Kari and her husband heard a loud banging. They got out of bed moments before the tornado blew the roof off their house and flung their bed into the

225

neighbor's trees. They knelt in prayer with their two children, and Kari thanked God for taking their house and sparing their lives. "Why did you thank God for taking our house?" her young daughter asked. "The Bible tells us to give thanks because this is God's will for us who are in Christ Jesus," Kari answered. "God loves us, and He's in control of our whole lives and has a purpose, a good purpose for taking our house." Then, with her own house a shambles, Kari set about helping her neighbors.[3]

These women are daughters of good character. They are joyful even in the midst of trouble, thankful even for disaster, and willing to serve others even when it is inconvenient. Like the noble woman of Proverbs 31, Kari teaches her children with wisdom, Elizabeth knows and fears God, and Stacy realizes that her body is less important than her soul.

Good character shines in moments of trouble (see Prov. 24:10), but it is built up in the everyday. The ability to respond with joy, patience, and thankfulness during trouble is not natural. It is learned—through example, instruction, discipline, and experience and through drawing near to God. Our daughters' good character will come from knowing what God wants them to know and doing what God wants them to do, from abiding in Jesus and practicing the habits of godliness. Then we will see our daughters respond to life with faith as Stacy and Elizabeth did and hear our daughters teach their children with wisdom as Kari did hers—and how happy we will be!

The Joy of Her Parents

Nine-year-old Jessica felt it was only fair that she hunt Easter eggs with children her own age, even though she is blind. But when the horn sounded, Jessica was left behind, and by the time she reached the field, all the eggs had been picked up. Then a boy standing nearby reached into his bag, took out an egg, and placed it on the ground near Jessica. When she found that one, he put two more on the ground. Soon, other children came and contributed an egg for Jessica to hunt.[4]

The boy who shared his eggs with Jessica may have done so because his father told him he should, but the joy Jessica's mother saw on his face indicated that he did it because *he* wanted to. The actions that come from within—from attitudes of generosity, patience, humility, repentance, and thankfulness—are what really make a parent glad.

Good character shows in what we do, but what we do comes from the heart. A daughter of good character is the joy of her parents (Prov. 23:15–16, 24–25; 29:17) and more valuable than riches or fame (31:10) because she wants to please God. When she is compelled not by fear of punishment or because her parents are looking over her shoulder but because her own heart motivates her to do what is right, it is the work of God (see Jer. 24:7; 31:33–34; Ezek. 11:19–20; Luke 6:45).

Application *Ask your daughter what kind of person she wants to be when she is old. What does she want people to remember most about her? What kind of reputation does she hope to have? Tell her what kind of person you hope she will be and why.*

The Work of God

You can help your daughter develop good habits, but God puts them in her heart. You can compel conformity on the outside, but God changes her on the inside. You can get her to do the right thing while you are watching, but God produces fruit that lasts (John 15:16).

Faith in Jesus Christ is the big box that contains all the qualities of good character.[5] Your daughter must live in Jesus to develop patience, kindness, a thankful heart, joy in times of trouble, love for others, and generosity (see John 15:1–17). True virtue comes only from true faith.[6] Good character is the inevitable result of knowing the triune God, for all three persons of the Trinity—Jesus, the Father, and the Holy Spirit—guarantee that your believing daughter will grow in godly attitudes and actions.

Jesus the Vine

"I am the vine; you are the branches," Jesus said (John 15:5). A branch produces fruit because it is connected to the vine; believers develop the fruit of the Spirit because they are united to Christ. Jesus is more than a model of good character; he is the source of good character. As the vine gives life to its branches, Jesus gives life to believers, and that life produces love, joy, peace, patience, kindness, goodness, faithfulness, humility, and self-control (Gal. 5:22–23). The fruit of the Spirit describe Jesus, and, like a vine to its branches, he imparts his own nature to us.

When your daughter believes, she is so united to Christ that his life becomes her life and all his blessings and benefits are hers. Jesus is not far off; he is within her (Col. 1:27) so that the power of his life is constantly available to her, constantly transforming her, constantly bringing her closer to what she really is. She grows in what she already has, the character of Christ.

God the Gardener

The Father is the good gardener (John 15:1). He plants the seed of holiness within us that grows into godly character, he weeds out the sins, and he cultivates the character of Jesus within us. He roots us in Christ (Col. 2:6–7) and then makes us grow (1 Cor. 3:6–7). He adopts us and grafts us into Christ (Rom. 11:17), and he prunes the branches so that they bear more fruit (John 15:2). Those he adopts as sons, he disciplines (Heb. 12:5–11) and purifies (Mal. 3:3–4; 1 Thess. 5:23–24; 1 Peter 1:3–7) so that they live as God's sons should (see, for example, Eph. 4:17–5:9; 1 John 2:6).

God is a patient farmer. He knows that your daughter's good character will not grow overnight. He is slow to anger and abounding in love; he remembers that she is dust (Ps. 103:8–18). As a faithful farmer, he tills, waters, fertilizes, protects her from harsh conditions, and drives away the pests and predators. She flourishes under his personal care. He takes care of the tender plant of your daughter's faith so that she remains in Christ and grows more like him (Rom. 8:29–30).

The Holy Spirit as Chemist

By some process we don't fully understand and can't duplicate, God made diamonds out of the same stuff as coal—yet what a difference between them! A lump of coal is soft, it rubs off on your hands, it is easily crushed or burned, and I never met anyone wearing a necklace made of coal. A diamond is the hardest substance we have, and one of the most valuable. Diamonds are useful, precious, and beautiful.

The change in a believer is as evident and undeniable as the difference between coal and diamonds, yet we are not able to explain fully how the Holy Spirit changes our hearts and minds. We don't completely understand how God works in us so that we willingly act according to his good pleasure (Phil. 2:13), how the good we do is the work of God and yet our own conscious choice, how we are completely dependent on God and yet not passive.

This is "the mysterious chemistry of the Holy Spirit,"[7] otherwise known as "the mystical union" with Christ. When your daughter is united to Jesus by the Holy Spirit, he lives in her and so changes and energizes her that she actually does become like Jesus in actions and attitudes.

The Holy Spirit Changes Her. The character of Jesus grows only in those who have been born again (John 3:3–8). A bad tree cannot bear good fruit. Grapes don't grow on thorn bushes. We don't pick figs off thistle plants or olives off fig trees (Matt. 7:16–18; James 3:11–12). To produce the fruit of good character, we must have a change in heart, from evil (Gen. 6:5; Rom. 3:23) to good (Ezek. 18:31; 36:25–27).

The Holy Spirit is the one who changes our hearts. We are born again of the Spirit and sanctified by the Spirit (Rom. 15:16; 2 Thess. 2:13; 1 Peter 1:2). He is "the bond by which Christ effectually unites us to himself" and the "secret energy . . . by which we come to enjoy Christ and all his benefits."[8] He applies the gospel in saving power to your daughter's soul. He makes her alive from her spiritual deadness, he subdues her rebellious will, he melts her hard heart, he opens her blind eyes, and he cleanses her from her sin.[9]

When your daughter is born again, the Holy Spirit gives her a new heart containing all the attributes of good character. Then, over time, he brings these attributes to expression in her attitudes and actions in ever-increasing fullness.

The Holy Spirit Energizes Her. The Holy Spirit is like the wind (John 3:8). We can't see the Spirit, but we can see his effect, just as we see trees bowing down in the wind or leaves dancing down an alley. We see the Holy Spirit's effect in the believer's conscious acts of faith (see 2 Cor. 1:22; 5:5; Phil. 2:12–13).[10]

The Holy Spirit renews your daughter's heart (John 3:5; Titus 3:5), mind (1 Cor. 2:6–16; 1 John 2:20), and will (Rom. 7:6; 8:5–17; Gal. 5:16–25) to press on toward the goal of her heavenly calling (Phil. 3:14). Through his "energizing activity,"[11] she wants to and will pray, read the Scriptures, obey God's commands, and love others. He creates a "continual flow of grace and power which produces fruit" so that she will abide in Christ, trust in the Word, obey it, and grow in good character.[12] He so changes her that she really feels, thinks, and acts according to his good purpose (Phil. 2:13).

If your daughter believes in Jesus, God himself has guaranteed that she will grow in good character. You don't have to be the perfect parent; she has a perfect Father in heaven who will discipline her, prune her, purify her, and encourage her. You don't have to be the perfect teacher; she has the Holy Spirit to teach her the truth. You don't have to provide the perfect environment for her; she is connected to Jesus, the true vine. This is good news for us parents—because none of us *can* be perfect.

If your daughter is not yet a believer, she needs Jesus. Good character and all the other benefits of salvation come from being connected to him by faith. Without this connection, she really can't develop the good character you want to see in her. You can't make her have faith; but you can pray that God would give her a new heart, and you can show her Jesus by the way you live, how you treat her, and what you teach her.

> **Application** *Read John 15:1–17 in family devotions. Talk about how a Christian's life is like that of a branch on a vine and how God is like a good gardener, cultivating good character in the Christian. Teach your daughter that when she believes in Jesus, she is united to Christ, tended by the Father, and changed and energized by the Holy Spirit.*

Teach Two Things

Whether your daughter already believes in Jesus or she has yet to come to faith, she needs to hear the gospel over and over again. She needs to learn about her sin and about God's grace. To grow in good character, she must understand the characteristics of sin and know the character of God. Use every opportunity to teach these two things.

The Characteristics of Sin

The foolish young man of Proverbs 7 didn't understand sin. He didn't recognize it in himself or the world. He didn't appreciate its strength and seduction. He didn't understand its dangers. He didn't see sin coming, he didn't realize how vulnerable he was to its allure, and he didn't foresee its consequences.

If your daughter doesn't understand sin, she will feel no need for Jesus. If she does not come to Jesus—both initially to save her and continually to keep her from temptation and give her the ability to do what is right—she will not grow in good character. So then, teach her the characteristics of sin.

Teach her that she is a sinner and she lives in a sinful world. Sin affects her emotions, thoughts, desires, actions, and body. It affects her neighbor and her boyfriend. It even affects the physical world around her. Every problem or trouble she has illustrates the effects of sin. Because of sin, she has wrong ideas, she feels unhappy, she can't do all the things she wants to do, she develops bad habits, she quarrels with her friends, and her body isn't perfect. Because of sin, her best friend lies to her, her teacher loses her temper, and her boyfriend acts selfishly. When she comes to you with her heartaches, problems, frustrations, and "Why did this happen?" questions, always show her how sin explains the troubles of this world.

Teach her to hate sin and resist temptation. Sin is breaking God's law in thought, word, or deed, and breaking God's law always has bad consequences. Sin masquerades as pleasure, but its end is always bitter. Sin has natural consequences, such as a drunk driver wrecking his car or a sexually active girl getting pregnant. In addition, God himself punishes sin, through emotional and psychological misery and ultimately in hell. Sin is destructive. "Sin is not a lesser degree of goodness, but a positive evil."[13] Don't allow your daughter to view sin casually, as if some sins didn't matter. Teach her that God hates all sin.

Teach her to recognize how sin lies, distorts, conceals, and misuses God's truth; how it hides the consequences, makes excuses, and blames others; how it makes bad choices seem good and bad situations seem harmless or fun. Show her how to evaluate what people say and what they ask her to do by what the Bible says about it. Can she think of someone in the Bible who thought, spoke, or acted this way? Did God approve or disapprove? What happened to that person? Did Jesus act or think this way? Does the Bible agree or disagree with this idea? Teach her that sin is seductive, but God's Word is true.

When you explain to your daughter how sin affects her and the world around her, never leave her there. *Always* point her toward God. The better your daughter understands God, the better she will understand the Bible, herself, others, and the world; the more easily she will recognize sin; and the more she will hate it and want to avoid it. A wise daughter, a daughter of good character, knows herself and the sin that so easily entangles her (Heb. 12:1), but she also knows the grace and power of God.

The Character of God

The better your daughter knows God, the more she will be happy, patient, wise, content in her circumstances, able to love others, aware of her sin, resting in God's forgiveness, and doing what is right by God's power. If you want good character to blossom in her, teach her who God is.

God is infinite, eternal, and unchangeable in his being, wisdom, power, holiness, justice, goodness, and truth.[14] He was not created. He doesn't depend on anything, and he doesn't need us to give him anything. He is already perfect, and he doesn't change. His power, wisdom, holiness, justice, goodness, and truth never diminish. He doesn't need to change his plans, because he knows everything and can do whatever he wants. He notices everything and forgets nothing (though he graciously chooses to remember our sin no more).

He has no moral blemish. All his attributes are holy, and everything that comes from him is good. Because God is patient and withholds his full wrath against sinners, we forget how much he hates sin in all its forms—thought or action, "little" or "big." We forget that he must punish even one failure to live up to his holy standards.

God is holy, but he is also love. He expressed his holiness and love by sending Jesus Christ to live a blameless life and die in our place. God punished our sin by placing it on Jesus on the cross and gave us Jesus' righteousness so that we could experience his great love.

He is faithful. He never lies. His love, mercy, and grace never fail. He is able to do all that he has promised, and he always does. We can rely on him. "No prayer is too hard for him to answer, no need too great for him to supply, no passion too strong for him to subdue, no temptation too powerful for him to deliver from, no misery too deep for him to relieve."[15]

To know this God, your daughter must be born again, born from above. The Holy Spirit must change her heart, renew her mind, and energize her actions. If you continually teach your daughter the characteristics of sin and the character of God, you will be presenting the gospel to her over and over. No matter how mature she becomes in her faith and good character, she will never outgrow the need to hear the good news—that God's grace through Jesus Christ is always greater than sin and always working in those who believe in him.

A daughter of good character knows what God wants her to know and does what God wants her to do. She loves God and serves others, avoids sin and develops good habits, uses her abilities to build God's kingdom, and knows her body is a temple of God. She grows in the fruit of the Spirit. She learns to be content with what God has given her. She gains wisdom, discipline, understanding, insight, prudence, and discretion. She listens to advice. She does what is right, just, and fair. She fears the Lord.

God develops this character in your daughter, but that doesn't mean you can go on a parenting hiatus. God uses you to form and develop your daughter's good character. Rest in his promises—and teach her daily. Thank God that you don't have to be a perfect parent—and pray that God would make you the parent you should be. Remember that God is at work in you as well as in your daughter. He will cause the seed he has planted in you and in her to grow and bear much fruit.

Application *Always have this question in mind:* How can I help my daughter know God better?

For Further Thought and Discussion

1. Read Jeremiah 24:7; 31:31–34; Ezekiel 11:19–20; 36:26–27; Matthew 5:21–28; 15:10–20; and Luke 6:45. What kinds of thoughts and actions come out of good hearts? Out of evil hearts? What makes a heart good or evil? Why are attitudes such as generosity, kindness, patience, humility, and thankfulness the truest signs of good character?

2. Read John 15:1–17. How is the Christian's life like that of a branch on a vine? What does the branch get from the vine? What do we get from Jesus? What fruit grows on the branch? What "fruit" grows in the Christian? How does being united to Christ guarantee that the fruit of good character will grow in the believer?

3. Read Psalms 1:1–3; 92:12–15; Isaiah 32:15; 60:21; John 15:1–2; and 1 Corinthians 3:6–9. Why do the righteous flourish and bear fruit? In what ways is God the good farmer? Why does the Father's personal care guarantee that the believer will grow?

4. Read John 3:5–8; Romans 8:5–27; 1 Corinthians 2:6–16; 2 Corinthians 1:21–22; 5:5; Galatians 5:16–25; and 1 Peter 1:1–2. How is the Holy Spirit like the wind? What is the Holy Spirit's "sanctifying work"? List the ways the Holy Spirit changes hearts, minds, and wills. In light of the Holy Spirit's sanctifying work, how should you pray for yourself? For your daughter?

5. How could you use the following situations to present your daughter with the gospel by teaching her about the characteristics of sin and the character of God?

   a. She comes home from school in tears because her best friend didn't sit with her on the bus.

   b. She hears that a student in another school shot a classmate, and she is afraid that will happen in her school.

c. Her boyfriend breaks up with her.

d. She says, "I'm so ugly!"

e. She asks if she can go to a party, and you find out there will be no chaperones.

f. You find out she has lied to you.

g. She gets detention at school.

h. She wants to buy a sexually provocative dress.

i. You are watching a movie on television that shows the characters having a sexual relationship outside of marriage.

j. Your next-door neighbor's teenage daughter becomes pregnant.

6. Think of other situations you have faced or might face with your daughter. How could you use them to present the gospel to her?

Notes

Chapter 1: What Your Daughter Needs

1 Melissa Healy, "Initiative to promote sexual abstinence," *The Los Angeles Times,* in *The Morning Call,* March 1, 1997, A25; "National Campaign Key Statistics," Campaign for Our Children, www.cfoc.org, May 1998.

2 Healy, "Initiative to promote sexual abstinence."

3 Maggie Gallagher, "Why Murphy Brown Is Winning," *The Wall Street Journal,* June 3, 1996, A14.

4 Ibid.

5 "Women and Drugs," *The Wall Street Journal,* June 6, 1996, A14; "Younger and Younger," *The Wall Street Journal,* March 5, 1997, A18.

6 Dianne Hales, "Early Bloomers," *Working Mother,* May 1998, 46.

7 Cynthia Crossen, "Growing Up Goes On and On," *The Wall Street Journal,* March 24, 1997, B7; see also Mary Pipher, *Reviving Ophelia: Saving the Selves of Adolescent Girls* (New York: Ballantine, 1974).

8 Pipher, *Reviving Ophelia,* 27.

9 Robert Frost, "The Road Not Taken," in *The Poetry of Robert Frost,* ed. Edward Connery Lathem (New York: Holt, Rhinehart and Winston, 1969), 105.

10 Dan Hartzell, "Remembering a lost soul," *The Morning Call,* July 26, 1997, B1, 9; Elliot Grossman, "Lawyer not surprised by Brader's death," *The Morning Call,* July 23, 1997, A8.

Chapter 2: Your Daughter and the World

1 Josh McDowell, "What is truth in today's world?" www.josh.org/rfw/josh.htm, January 29, 2000.

2 The chief end of man and woman is to glorify God and enjoy him forever (Westminster Shorter Catechism, Q. 1).

3 Mary Pipher, *Reviving Ophelia: Saving the Selves of Adolescent Girls* (New York: Ballantine, 1974), 97–99.

4 Douglas Kelly and Philip Rollinson, *The Westminster Shorter Catechism in Modern English* (Phillipsburg, N.J.: P&R, 1986).

5 Pipher, *Reviving Ophelia*, 184. See also 54–57.

6 Glenn Frey, Jack Tempchin, Danny Kortchmar, "Love in the Twenty-first Century," MCA Records, 1993.

7 Maggie Gallagher, "Why Murphy Brown Is Winning," *The Wall Street Journal*, June 3, 1996, A14.

8 "Teen Moms," *The Wall Street Journal*, May 8, 1998, A14.

9 *Catechism for Young Children: An Introduction to the Shorter Catechism* (Horsham, Pa.: Great Commission Publications, 1991).

10 Pipher, *Reviving Ophelia*, 17–28, 93–95.

11 Michael Ryan, " 'If You Can't Teach Me, Don't Criticize Me,' " *Parade*, May 11, 1997, 6–7.

Chapter 3: Show Her the Right Way

1 L. Berkhof, *Systematic Theology*, 4th ed. (Grand Rapids: Eerdmans, 1977), 251.

2 J. Douma, *The Ten Commandments: Manual for the Christian Life*, trans. Nelson D. Kloosterman (Phillipsburg, N.J.: P&R, 1996), 166.

3 Some biblical counselors are reluctant to speak of love or affection as a human "need." But in a less strict sense of the word, your daughter "needs" hugs. If she is not hugged by her parents, it may take an exceptional measure of God's grace (in the form of friends, Christian fellowship, or a very caring husband) to make up for an early lack of human affection.

4 Robert S. Mavis, "Absence of fathers the root of many of nation's troubles," *The Morning Call*, August 16, 1997, B21.

Chapter 5: Instill the Right Habits

1 See L. Berkhof, *Systematic Theology*, 4th ed. (Grand Rapids: Eerdmans, 1977), 533.

2 Taken from Byron Jay Peters, "Devotions: The Daily Difference," unpublished handout, 1995.

Chapter 6: Remember She Is Foolish

1 This definition of wisdom comes from Sunday school material developed by Great Commission Publications.

2 Merrill F. Unger, *Unger's Bible Dictionary*, 3rd ed. (Chicago: Moody, 1978), 375.

3 See James T. Draper, Jr., *Proverbs: Practical Directions for Living* (Wheaton, Ill.: Tyndale, 1977), 11–14, 20.

4 William J. Bennett, *The Children's Book of Virtues* (New York: Simon & Schuster, 1995), inside cover, 6.

5 John Rosemond, "Teen's foolishness will run its course if parents do job well," *The Morning Call*, April 4, 1996, E6.

6 Draper, *Proverbs*, 53.

7 Lisa Miller, "This Spring Break, The Hottest Thing Is Unprotected Skin," *The Wall Street Journal*, March 7, 1997, A1, 6.

8 L. Berkhof, *Systematic Theology*, 4th ed. (Grand Rapids: Eerdmans, 1977), 255.

9 Dan Hartzell, "Youth killed by storekeeper in robbery try," *The Morning Call*, December 16, 1996, A1.

10 Aminah Franklin, "Being in older crowd was 'cool,' " *The Morning Call*, December 17, 1996, A1.

Chapter 7: Teach Her to Love God and Hate Sin

1 Robert Frost, "The Road Not Taken," in *The Poetry of Robert Frost*, ed. Edward Connery Lathem (New York: Holt, Rhinehart and Winston, 1969), 105.

Chapter 8: Teach Her to Make Wise Choices

1 Carol Bishop Hipps, "Kudzu," *Horticulture*, June/July 1994, 36–39.

2 Josh McDowell, "What is truth in today's world?" www.josh.org/rfw/josh.htm, January 29, 2000.

3 John Frame, course syllabus. Since I took this course, Frame has written much of his course material into his *Doctrine of the Knowledge of God* (Phillipsburg, N.J.: P&R, 1987) and *Perspectives on the Word of God: An Introduction to Christian Ethics* (Phillipsburg, N.J.: P&R, 1990).

Chapter 9: She Is the Image of God

1 Mary Pipher, *Reviving Ophelia: Saving the Selves of Adolescent Girls* (New York: Ballantine, 1994), 11–28; see also Nicky Marone, *How to Father a Successful Daughter* (New York: Ballantine, 1988), 3–6.

2 Cynthia Crossen, "Growing Up Goes On and On and On," *The Wall Street Journal*, March 24, 1997, B1, 9.

3 Marone, *How to Father a Successful Daughter*, 7.

4 *Catechism for Young Children: An Introduction to the Shorter Catechism* (Horsham, Pa.: Great Commission Publications, 1991), Qq. 1–5.

5 G. I. Williamson, *The Westminster Confession of Faith for Study Classes* (Philadelphia: P&R, 1964), 43.

6 Ibid., 25.

7 Westminster Shorter Catechism, Q. 4.

8 *Catechism for Young Children*, Q. 9.

9 See L. Berkhof, *Systematic Theology*, 4th ed. (Grand Rapids: Eerdmans, 1977), 192, 195–96, 204–5; Meredith Kline, *Images of the Spirit* (Grand Rapids: Baker, 1980), 30.

10 John Calvin, *Institutes of the Christian Religion*, ed. John T. McNeill (Philadelphia: Westminster Press, 1960), 1.15.3. For an in-depth look at the glory image of God in man, see Kline, *Images of the Spirit*, 9–34.

11 Berkhof, *Systematic Theology*, 207; Francis Turretin, *Institutes of Elenctic Theology*, 3 vols. (Phillipsburg, N.J.: P&R, 1992, 1994, 1997), 1:465.

12 Williamson, *Westminster Confession*, 25.

13 Susan T. Foh, *Women and the Word of God* (Phillipsburg, N.J.: P&R, 1979), 175; see 175–77; 58–61.

14 See Turretin, *Institutes of Elenctic Theology*, 1:469.

15 Although Jesus and the Father are equal (one) (John 1:1, 14; 10:30; 14:6–9), the Father is "the head of Christ" (1 Cor. 11:3) in Jesus' function as Savior (John 4:34; 6:38; 1 Cor. 15:20–28; Phil. 2:5–8; Heb. 10:5–7). The husband is the head of his wife as the functional head of two equals (1 Cor. 11:3, 8–12). For more on the equality of man and woman, see chapter 10. For more on submitting and helping in marriage, see chapter 16.

Chapter 10: She Can Be a "Son" of God

1 *Catechism for Young Children: An Introduction to the Shorter Catechism* (Horsham, Pa.: Great Commission Publications, 1991), Q. 21.

2 Francis Turretin, *Institutes of Elenctic Theology*, 3 vols. (Phillipsburg, N.J.: P&R, 1992, 1994, 1997), 1:466.

3 L. Berkhof, *Systematic Theology*, 4th ed. (Grand Rapids: Eerdmans, 1977), 207.

4 John Calvin, *Institutes of the Christian Religion*, ed. John T. McNeill (Philadelphia: Westminster Press, 1960), 2.2.12.

5 See Susan T. Foh, *Women and the Word of God* (Phillipsburg, N.J.: P&R, 1979), 67–69.

6 Calvin, *Institutes*, 2.1.3.

7 Meredith Kline, *Images of the Spirit* (Grand Rapids: Baker, 1980), 23.

8 See John Murray, *Redemption Accomplished and Applied* (1955; Grand Rapids: Eerdmans, 1980); Turretin, *Institutes of Elenctic Theology*, 2:266–69.

9 John W. Sanderson, *The Fruit of the Spirit* (1972; reprint Phillipsburg, N.J.: P&R, 1985), 34, 178.

10 Cynthia Crossen, "Growing Up Goes On and On," *The Wall Street Journal*, March 24, 1997, B1, 9; Dianne Hales, "Early Bloomers," *Working Mother*, May 1998, 45. Interestingly, researchers have found that the risk of ovarian cancer is directly related to a woman's number of lifetime ovulations or menstrual cycles (Paul Recer, "Study: Have babies, avoid ovarian cancer," Associated Press, in *The Morning Call*, July 2, 1997, A7). So then, girls who menstruate earlier may also have a higher incidence of cancer.

11 *Unger's Bible Dictionary* (Chicago: Moody, 1978), 1080–82; *Pictorial Bible Dictionary* (Grand Rapids: Zondervan, 1972), 834–36.

12 Mary Pipher, *Reviving Ophelia: Saving the Selves of Adolescent Girls* (New York: Ballantine, 1994), 69–70.

Chapter 11: She Can Be Happy Serving God and Others

1 These girls are described by Mary Pipher, *Reviving Ophelia: Saving the Selves of Adolescent Girls* (New York: Ballantine, 1994).

2 Janet Chase, *Daughters of Change: Growing Up Female in America* (Boston: Little, Brown, 1981), 163.

3 See John Calvin, *Institutes of the Christian Religion*, ed. John T. McNeill (Philadelphia: Westminster Press, 1960), 2.1.2., 2.2.11.

4 Nicky Marone, *How to Father a Successful Daughter* (New York: Ballantine, 1988), 263.

5 L. Berkhof, *Systematic Theology*, 4th ed. (Grand Rapids: Eerdmans, 1977), 515.

6 All unhappiness and depression are caused by sin, but not always the sins of the individual. Remember that the Fall affected the body and the world as well as the soul. Some depressions and other mental problems have underlying physical causes. If your daughter has ongoing, deep depression not overcome by examining her conscience and repenting of any sins she knows she has committed, take her to a physician for a physical examination.

7 J. I. Packer, *Knowing God* (Downers Grove, Ill.: InterVarsity, 1973), 102–3.

8 A *shalwar chemise* is similar to a pantsuit, with very loose pants and a long tunic. It's less formal than the *sari*.

9 "Forum: How has taking an overseas trip changed your ministry perspective?" *Bright Side*, October 1997, 2.

10 Ibid.

Chapter 12: She Can Learn to Do Something Well

1 Sophia Lezin, "Drive and determination," *The Morning Call*, September 14, 1997, B1, 2.

2 Melanie Novak, "Confidence and discipline: Karate helps prepare girls for adolescence and leadership," *The Morning Call*, December 15, 1996, B1, 8.

3 Michael Pearce, "My Daughter, My Hunting Buddy," *The Wall Street Journal*, April 15, 1997, A16.

4 See Mary Pipher, *Reviving Ophelia: Saving the Selves of Adolescent Girls* (New York: Ballantine, 1994), 265–67.

5 See Nicky Marone, *How to Father a Successful Daughter* (New York: Ballantine, 1988), 171–84.

6   For questions to ask about your daughter's strengths and how they fit into broad job categories, see Raelynne P. Rein and Rachael Rein, *How to Develop Your Child's Gifts and Talents During the Elementary Years* (Los Angeles: Lowell House, 1994).

7   See Richard Nelson Bolles, *What Color Is Your Parachute? A Practical Manual for Job-Hunters and Career-Changers* (Berkeley, Calif.: Ten Speed Press, 1998).

8   Sally Squires, "Athletic teen females less sexually active," Washington Post, in *The Morning Call*, June 7, 1998, H3.

9   Mary Pipher, "Surviving Toxic Media: How the Church Can Help," *UUA World Magazine*, January/February 1998, UU World.htm.

Chapter 13: She Can Like Her Body

1   Gary R. Blockus, "The Perfect Outlook," *The Morning Call*, June 21, 1998, A1, 2; Elizabeth Shepard, " 'Confidence Is the Sexiest Thing a Woman Can Have,' " *Parade*, June 21, 1998, 8–10; Pete Leffler, "A Model Life," *The Morning Call*, December 3, 1998, A1, 12, 13.

2   Mary Pipher, *Reviving Ophelia: Saving the Selves of Adolescent Girls* (New York: Ballantine, 1994), 29–32.

3   Pipher, *Reviving Ophelia*, 32, 146–47; Joan Jacobs Brumberg, *The Body Project: An Intimate History of American Girls* (New York: Random House, 1997), xxi, xxiv, 122–23, 126–28; "Study finds men happier than women with the way they look," Washington Post, in *The Morning Call*, May 26, 1998, D1.

4   Brumberg, *The Body Project*, xxiv.

5   Carol J. Eagle and Carol Colman, *All That She Can Be: Helping Your Daughter Achieve Her Full Potential and Maintain Her Self-Esteem During the Critical Years of Adolescence* (New York: Simon & Schuster, 1993), 46, 49–50; Dianne Hales, "Early Bloomers," *Working Mother*, May 1998, 44–49.

6   Pipher, *Reviving Ophelia*, 97–98.

7   See Brumberg, *The Body Project*, 5.

8   Pipher, *Reviving Ophelia*, 56, 184; Bart Jones, "Becoming Miss Venezuela means 9-month boot camp," Associated Press, in *The Morning Call*, November 23, 1997, A12.

9   Brumberg, *The Body Project*, xxiv–xxv, 97.

10   John W. Sanderson, *The Fruit of the Spirit* (1972; reprint Phillipsburg, N.J.: P&R, 1985), 175.

11   As late as the 1970s, in South Korea full-figured women were considered more sexually attractive, but as Western advertising and programming became more prominent, the standard changed. By the 1990s, eating disorders had appeared, the weight-loss industry was booming, and even elementary school girls were dieting (Sonni Efron, "Asian doctors report rise in eating disorders," Los Angeles Times, in *The Morning Call*,

October 19, 1997, A12). A similar change took place in Egypt, but over an even shorter time; see Amy Dockser Marcus, "It's Not Easy Being Lean in Cairo Today, But Women Do Try," *The Wall Street Journal*, March 4, 1998, A1, 8.

12 Brumberg, *The Body Project*, 66, photo insert 9 caption, photo insert 25 caption.

13 Yumiko Ono, "Fashion's New Queens: Heavy Teens," *The Wall Street Journal*, July 31, 1998, B1, 4.

14 Brumberg, *The Body Project*, xxii, 118, 182, 197.

15 Hales, "Early Bloomers," 48.

16 Brumberg, *The Body Project*, 16–25.

17 Stacey Kole, "Satisfying Starving Souls," *Bright Side*, November 1998, 3.

Chapter 14: She Must Develop Sexual Self-Control

1 Eun-Kyung Kin, "Teen pot use up," Associated Press, in *The Morning Call*, August 22, 1998, A39; Michael J. McCarthy, "States Restrict Teen Drivers to Curb Deaths," *The Wall Street Journal*, November 11, 1996, B1; "National Campaign Key Statistics," Campaign for Our Children, www.cfoc.org, May 1998.

2 "U.S. high schoolers just saying no . . . ," Associated Press, in *The Morning Call*, September 18, 1998, A12.

3 Quotations in this section from " 'Oh, No, I Can't Get Pregnant': Teen Parents Talk About What They've Learned," *Parade*, June 14, 1998, 24–26; "You Can Only *Really* Get to Know Someone by Living Together—Yes or No?," *Parade*, October 19, 1997, 17; Mary Pipher, *Reviving Ophelia: Saving the Selves of Adolescent Girls* (New York: Ballantine, 1994), 34, 215.

4 John W. Sanderson, *The Fruit of the Spirit* (1972; reprint Phillipsburg, N.J.: P & R, 1985), 140.

5 "National Campaign Key Statistics."

6 "Ten Tips for Parents to Help Their Children Avoid Teen Pregnancy," Campaign for Our Children, www.cfoc.org, May 1998.

7 Ibid.

8 "Partners, Predators, Peers, Protectors: Males and Teen Pregnancy," Child Trends, www.childtrends.org, May 1998; "National Campaign Key Statistics."

9 Josh McDowell seminar, "Maximum Sex."

10 Robert Wolgemuth, "Just Keep Talking: Fathers and daughters who converse together stay together," *Focus on the Family*, October 1996.

11 Dianne Hales, "How Teenagers See Things," *Parade*, August 18, 1996, 4–5; Michael J. McManus, "Encouraging Chastity," in *The Morning Call*, September 27, 1998, B31.

Chapter 15: Teach Her to Be Wise in Dating

1 Mike Royko, "A chat in basement might have averted a slap in the face," Tribune Media Services, in *The Morning Call*, September 10, 1996, A15.
2 Mary Pipher, *Reviving Ophelia: Saving the Selves of Adolescent Girls* (New York: Ballantine, 1995), 34–35.
3 "National Campaign Key Statistics," Campaign for Our Children, www.cfoc.org, May 1998.
4 Conference speech, March 22, 1997.
5 "Partners, Predators, Peers, Protectors: Males and Teen Pregnancy," Child Trends, www.childtrends.org, May 1998.
6 Ibid.
7 Pipher, *Reviving Ophelia*, 99, 123–24, 211.

Chapter 16: Teach Her God's Way of Marriage

1 Mort Walker, April 17, 1996.
2 Hadley Arkes, "Finding Fault with No-Fault," *The Wall Street Journal*, April 16, 1996, A12.
3 The head of the National Organization of Single Mothers, Andrea Engber, says, "There are very few women who are like, 'I've got this Alan-Alda-diaper-changing man but I'm just not going to marry him.' If they could wave a wand and have Mr. Right, they would. But what they're doing is not settling for Mr. Adequate" (Michelle Boorstein, "Single, with children," Associated Press, in *The Morning Call*, September 13, 1998, E2).
4 George F. Will, "Get rid of marriage textbooks, have students study great authors," Washington Post Writers Group, in *The Morning Call*, November 10, 1998, A11.
5 Boorstein, "Single, with children."
6 *Let Me Be a Woman* (Wheaton, Ill.: Tyndale, 1976), 78.
7 Connie Lauerman, "Counseling makes couples learn ropes before tying knot," *Chicago Tribune*, in *The Morning Call*, June 26, 1997, D6.
8 Scripture clearly teaches that man and woman are equal. Both are the image of God (Gen. 1:27), both are to fill the earth and rule over it (1:28–30), and both become "sons" and heirs of God (Gal. 3:26–4:7). Scripture also clearly teaches that headship and submission can happen between equals. Note that "the head of Christ is God [the Father]" (1 Cor. 11:3). Jesus is equal (one with) the Father (John 1:1, 14; 10:30; 14:6–9), yet in his function as Savior, Jesus also submitted to the Father (John 4:34; 6:38; Luke 22:42; Phil. 2:5–8; Heb. 10:5–7; see also 1 Cor. 15:20–28).
9 James T. Draper, *Proverbs: Practical Directions for Living* (Wheaton, Ill.: Tyndale, 1971), 147; see also 147–52.

Chapter 17: A Daughter of Good Character

1 Stacy James, "Choose Joy," *Bright Side*, October 1998, 3.

2 Elizabeth J. Davis, "Brought from the East," *New Horizons*, July 1998, 10–11.

3 Kari Maggard, "God's Next Thing," *Bright Side*, May 1998, 3.

4 "Dear Abby," in *The Morning Call*, May 5, 1998, D3.

5 John W. Sanderson, *The Fruit of the Spirit* (1972; reprint Phillipsburg, N.J.: P&R, 1985), 144–52.

6 John Calvin, *Institutes of the Christian Religion*, ed. John T. McNeill (Philadelphia: Westminster Press, 1977), 3.14.3.

7 Sanderson, *Fruit of the Spirit*, 34, 178.

8 Calvin, *Institutes*, 3.1.1.

9 Arthur W. Pink, *The Attributes of God* (Grand Rapids: Baker, 1975), 70.

10 See L. Berkhof, *Systematic Theology*, 4th ed. (Grand Rapids: Eerdmans, 1977, 449–50.

11 John Murray, *Redemption Accomplished and Applied* (1955; Grand Rapids: Eerdmans, 1980), 147, 150.

12 Sanderson, *Fruit of the Spirit*, 29.

13 Berkhof, *Systematic Theology*, 232.

14 Westminster Shorter Catechism, Q. 4. For much of the material that follows, I am indebted to Pink, *The Attributes of God*.

15 Pink, *Attributes of God*, 51.